32 Days with Abraham

By

Mark R. Etter

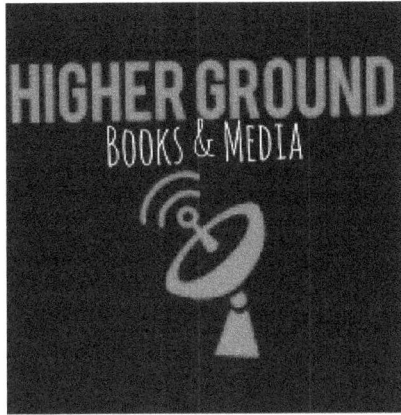

Higher Ground Books & Media
Springfield, Ohio.
http://highergroundbooksandmedia.com

Printed in the United States of America 2018

32 Days with Abraham

By

Mark R. Etter

DEDICATION

This book is dedicated to my wife Joan who has been my "Sarah" on my journey through life.

Table of Contents

32 Days Series

This series of devotional books is designed to be a tool that

brings you closer to Christ. The devotions are designed to

have depth so that you dig below the surface and understand

the context. Each devotion is based on a single scripture

passage and lays out the events in an organized way to help

you comprehend the deeper meanings in the passage and

then apply them to your life. As a free gift to you, there are

included in this book twelve bible studies that are meant to be

shared. You have my permission to copy the student guides

for your church or small group bible studies. Each bible study

is connected to one of the devotions and to a leader's guide

so that you can feel confident leading others to understand

God's word. My hope is that you enjoy these devotions and

studies and let the Holy Spirit change your life through them.

Read the Bible passage for each devotion and feel free to

read the devotions several times as you ponder the message

for your life. The twelve bible studies and leader's guides may

also lead you to greater understanding of those texts. God is ready to sit down with you through these devotions and

change your life.

Abraham Introduction

Abraham's features have been recorded in stain glass and chiseled into life-like statues. He has become one of the super heroes of the Bible. We imagine men and women like Abraham and Sarah as extraordinary men and women who have more courage and character that we could ever have in our life. How could we ever be like them? How could we ever have that kind of faith or temperament in our lives? The pages of the Bible may surprise you with the truth. Abraham is not a "superman". He is a man taken from obscurity and polished by the Lord. The Bible doesn't hold back but shows us the real man. It shows us a man named Abram who failed on many occasions. He only becomes the man of God that we honor because of the teaching and testing of a God who loves him. The Bible doesn't hide Abraham's failures, but shows us the whole story so that we can follow the journey of Abraham and become a man or woman of God like him.

Think of Abraham's story as a pattern for what could happen if you were willing to let the Lord teach you. Learn the lessons that Abraham learned through his life. See how his faith guided him and how your faith can be the key to having the blessings that Abraham received from God. God wants to teach every Christian these lessons so that they can be a person of faith and blessing. Your life will not be identical to Abraham's but will follow a path that the Lord has chosen specifically for you. If you follow the Lord, as Abraham does, you can have God's blessing and be a blessing to others. Don't get discouraged by your failures but seek to learn from them as Abraham did.

My goal in these devotions is for you to follow Abraham and learn some of the lessons that the Lord taught him. He began as an ordinary person like you or I. It was God who made him great. This same God wants to shape your faith through His scripture so that you can enjoy many of the blessings that Abraham did. God bless you and may you be a blessing to others as Abraham has become a blessing to you and to me.

1. Seeing the Value Underneath
Gen. 12:1

Context: After describing His dealings with man in the flood and the tower of Babel, we now see God deal in grace with a single man. The rest of Genesis will follow the story of Abraham and his descendants as God unveils His plan for salvation and shows His great love for mankind.

He almost missed it. Buried on the yard sale table was a tarnished tea pot amidst an array of ceramic vases and chipped glasses. It hardly looked like it was worth the five-dollar price that the owner had put on it. Yet, when he saw it, John immediately picked it up and weighed it in his hands. He scanned its tarnished surface and after a second or two knew that he had a hidden treasure. Quietly, he paid the young girl manning the cash box and headed to his car with the tea pot and a few other items.

At home, he used a small hammer to work out the dings that marred the surface of the tea pot and returned the gentle curve to the surface. He found his tin of silver polish and began to clean years of tarnish off the surface with a series of gentle strokes. His wife thought he was crazy for spending so much time on a worthless old pot. Yet, as the layers of grime slowly came off, the reason John has treasured this pot became apparent. The name of its maker, Paul Revere, was engraved on the bottom. What the world had seen and discarded as a worthless pot was a valuable piece of history that John had affectionately restored.

The first chapters of Genesis record one failure after another for mankind. A perfect couple is created by God only to fall into sin and begin to accuse each other. Their first children are born, and the first murder is recorded after a number of years have passed. The world continues down this path of sin and corruption until God finds it necessary to cleanse His world by a flood. Even the flood cannot stop the rebellion as man begins to build a tower that will reach to the skies. A casual reader of these early chapters of Genesis would wonder what God was going to do with the human race. Should He destroy mankind and start again? The answer is that God has a different idea of how to create a people for himself.

God called a man and wife to leave their home so that God might give humanity a new beginning. Abram and Sarai were not perfect by any means. Like the silver pot they were tarnished. Joshua 24:2 reminds us that Abram's family worshipped other gods when it says, "*Long ago your forefathers, including Terah the father of Abraham and Nahor, lived beyond the River and worshiped other gods*" Yet, the Lord called him (Acts 7:2) at a time when he was living in Ur of the Chaldeans. God called him from this great city of wealth and culture. God called him from a city that was devoted to the moon goddess. God called Abram to follow and make a new start that would change the world. Like the tea pot, God saw something in this tarnished pot of a man and took him to be His own.

For Abram to be useful to God, he needed to be polished. He needed the tarnish to be taken slowly off his life. God did that by calling Abram to "*Leave your country*" He was to leave that place of idolatry where the moon god was worshipped. He was to leave this place of money and power. He was to leave this comfortable place where it would be so easy to fall back into the old habits that were so much a part of this world. The world that Abram grew up in ran counter to the values of the Lord. Abram could not live there and create a new life with the Lord. He could not keep one foot in this world of idols and fast living and try to live a new life for the Lord.

The call of Abram is a call for us. Our God does not expect us to be polished when we come to Him. He does want us to be willing to leave things as we cling to Him. He wants in a place where we can be polished and made new. Over the next thirty-one days, we will follow the life of Abraham and see the process of that polishing. We will see how the Lord wants to challenge us and change us. It may get a little uncomfortable at times but take time to stop and think about the lessons from Abraham's life. You will see Abraham at his best and at his worst. You will see that this great man became great only because he allowed the Lord to work in his life. You will have a glimpse of what you can be when the master takes the tarnish off your life and exposes the person that he created underneath. Our goal is summarized in 2 Cor. 5:17, *"Therefore if anyone is in Christ, he is a new creation; the old has gone, the new has come."*

- What would you like your life to look like as God takes

  away the tarnish?

2. God's Dreams for You
Gen. 12: 2-9

Context: The call goes out to Abram while he is still in Ur to follow the Lord. While Genesis 1-11 followed the story of God's dealings with the world, Chapter 12 begins the story of God's gracious dealings with one man and his descendants.

My children are grown now, but I remember as they grew, my wife and I had dreams for them all. We wanted them to stay close to the Lord, find a great spouse and work in an area that brought fulfillment to their life. I am sure that you have such dreams for yourself and for your children. Did you realize that God has dreams for you as well? Our heavenly Father has dreams for each of us. Often those dreams are greater than we can imagine. Such were the dreams that God had for Abram. Little did this man from Ur dream what he would become in God's hands.

The man from Ur seems average and yet God saw much more in him. The first promise seems almost daunting, *"I will make you into a great nation and I will bless you." (v.2)* A man and wife come to a strange land and God promises to make him great. Today, Abraham is a person that Jews, Christians and Muslims all think about as their father. He is a model and life example for all of us. As we meet him, Abram is not yet that man. God will mold His servant and give him character. God will bless the foreigner and make him someone that his neighbors consider a mighty prince (Gen. 23:5). God will do for Abram and for us what no man can do for themselves. He will make us great by changing our character and our future.

God will take this stranger and make him a blessing to everyone that has or will ever live. Think about the scope of that promise, *"and all peoples on earth will be blessed through you." (v.3)* Surely, every American could say that we are blessed by the work of Washington or Lincoln. Yet, few in Africa or Asia could say that they were blessed by these men. Through Jesus who is the descendant of Abram, everyone in the world has been blessed. The death and resurrection of Jesus changes the possible future of every living person. God will take this ordinary man and make him the beginning of a movement that will change the history of the world. Abram's faith and life will inspire many and be an example that many will follow.

Ur was a great and prosperous city. Archaeology has shown that the city was a great civilization. Canaan was more like the American West with few comforts and conveniences. Abram and Sarai gave up the luxury of Ur to follow God's command. Yet the Lord promises that as much as Abram has lost, his descendants will gain even more. *"To your offspring, I will give this land."(v. 7)* He has left a city, he will gain a country and a home. He has left the prosperity of Ur, but he will have great wealth and honor in this new place. All that Abram has left, the Lord will fill with new blessings. His willingness to follow God would open the door for the Lord to bless him in ways that he never imagined.

God's dreams for you and me are big, too. The plans that the Lord pours out for his people in scripture are amazing. Few Christians realize those dreams, however. The reason is that, like Abram, you have to follow God. You will not get to your destination if you do not follow the directions on the map or the GPS. Likewise, the Christian will not have God's plans for him if he is not willing to follow the Lord's ways and character. All of the promises given to Abram were possible because he left his country, people and family. We must be willing to obey the Lord as He shapes us and removes the tarnish from our lives or the dreams will not come true. This may seem daunting, but the life of Abram will show that it is possible.

What would your life look like if it followed God's plan? Imagine if you had a character that people around you admired and were willing to follow? Imagine being a blessing to your family, to your friends, and to your coworkers? It is not too late to start. Abram was 75 years old (Gen. 12:4) when the adventure began. He had come from a family that had worshipped false gods in Ur. You may think that God's dreams for you could never come true. Don't underestimate the power and love of our God. The life of Abram shows what is possible and it shows that it is possible because God loves you. New life is available to everyone. We have a God who can work miracles even with us.

- Of the promises that God made to Abram, which would you long for God to give to you? Why?

3. Trusting or Scheming
Genesis 12:10-20

Context: This is Abram's first test and first failure. He leaves a famine and seems to leave God behind as well. He fails to trust the Lord's promise of protection resulting in great pain for his family and others.

Should you panic or pray? Somehow, those seem to be the two choices available to me when problems come. I wish that I could tell you that I usually pick prayer, but I find that I am more like Abram in our text. Trusting God is not the first reaction that most of us have. We find ourselves in a problem and we panic. What will I do? We come up with a plan hoping that it will work. In the meantime, it is easy to leave God completely behind. We want to trust things that we can see and control rather than pray and trust an unseen God. The result is that, like Abram, our ways cause us more problems. God alone has the answers that we need if we will trust Him.

There is no record that Abram ever faced a famine in Ur or in Haran. Yet, the first test of his faith after receiving the wonderful promises comes in the form of a famine. His solution is simple. *"Now there was a famine in the land, and Abram went down to Egypt."* (v.10) **Sadly**, Abram leaves the place that the Lord has called him to and goes to a foreign land. In the text, God has just promised to bless him and to be with him. God had given Abram this land and a future, but Abram leaves it all at the first sign of trouble. We don't even read that he prayed or consulted God before he made his decision. He saw that the land south of Palestine had food and he decided that he would abandon God's land as part of his solution.

Abram's solution is not without problems. Having feared the famine, somewhere along the journey he began to fear the Egyptians. His wife is beautiful, and he fears that the people of this strange land will kill him to have Sarai as their own. He has not learned to trust the Lord yet and so he comes up with another solution. He tells Sarai to *"Say you are my sister."(v.13)* His fear and selfishness will put his wife and the future of all God's promises in danger as he seeks to protect himself. His lies bring greater danger to Sarai and himself. Sarai is taken to the harem of the Pharaoh. His solutions begin to unravel.

It is God who has to rescue Abram. The Lord made promises that He intended to fulfill. The birth of Isaac to Sarai will not happen if Sarai is in the harem of the Pharaoh. While Abram was supposed to be a blessing to the world, he would become a curse to Pharaoh. In order that Abram's lie might be exposed, *"the Lord inflicted serious diseases on Pharaoh and his household." (v.17)* Ironically, Abram has sinned, but it is the Egyptians who will pay the penalty. God's curse opens Pharaoh's eyes so that Sarai is returned. The story ends with Abram being thrown out of Egypt so that he must trust God to deliver him from the famine.

Our first response in times of crisis should be to pray and not to plot or worry till we have our own solution. Danger should draw us to the Lord rather than push us away from Him. Sadly, we often figure out what we think is the best solution and if that solution doesn't work well, we may turn to the Lord in prayer to beg God to make our solution work. Perhaps, Abram finally prayed to God when Sarai is bound for the harem. Weeping over the pain he has caused Sarai and himself, he thinks of the promises of his God and confesses his sin. Maybe, it was on his knees that he finally realized that only the Lord can save him.

The story could have ended differently. The famine could have come on the land, but in this scenario, Abram prays to the Lord. It is not hard to imagine that the Lord would have provided for Abram and his herds by shortening the famine or even leading Abram to a place where the grass was plentiful. In this scenario, Sarai is never taken to the harem and the promises of God are never in danger. The famine would have taught Abram to depend on the Lord in prayer and trust God in every difficulty. It is the path that we should seek. Real solutions come to those who seek the Lord. God may not give us exactly what we want, but He will bring us through each trial. Troubles teach those who turn to God that we can depend on our God and His love. Trusting God beats scheming every time. Our God can do what we are unable to do.

- What problem has caused you to panic? How would prayer have changed the outcome?

4. Humble Choices
Genesis 13: 1-13

Context: Departing Egypt, Abram returns to the place between Bethel and Ai where he had built an altar to the Lord. Great wealth gained in Egypt forces Abram and Lot to separate as Abram demonstrates humility and generosity to his nephew.

Money can wreck a family. I have watched children fight over their parent's inheritance even before the funeral is over. I have seen husbands and wives fight over the checkbook. All of us have seen a child pout when he can't have a toy he saw on television or in the store. It is all about selfishness. We don't care who gets slighted as long as we get what we want. When Christians have disputes like that, the reputation of the Lord suffers. The outside world looks at those families and wonders why anyone would want to be a Christian. People notice the conflict and miss the acts of loving kindness done by Christians. One battle can keep dozens of people away from the grace of our loving God.

Abram and Lot left Egypt as wealthy men. The pharaoh

had given them flocks, servants and camels. When they
returned, their success caused a new problem; *"the land
would not support them." (v.6)* The land simply could no longer
handle their combined wealth. I imagine the herdsmen arguing
over the choice pieces of pasture. The disputes become a test
for Abram. Just as God had sent the famine to test Abram's
faith, this becomes a test of Abram's character. How will he
resolve the conflict? Will he show that he has grown in Godly
character? Like all of us, he must deal with the problems that
come with success. The great wealth has caused a rift in the
family and a dispute that just won't go away.

Abram is determined to be a peacemaker. Family was
obviously important to Abram and Lot was his only family
member. He tells Lot, *"Let's not have any quarreling between
you and me." (v.8)* He could have ordered Lot and his
herdsman to change their behavior as the senior member of
the group, but he has a better idea. Instead of dividing the
land and ordering Lot and his men to take the share he gives
them, he humbly lets Lot make the choice of how the land will
be divided. The land before them is great and there is no

reason to fight. Furthermore, Abram has faith and trusts the Lord to bless him and take care of him no matter which piece of land he receives. A proud man would have divided the family for his own gain; Abram shows humility and prevents a rift in the family with his selfless act.

Lot seized the opportunity and grabbed what he considered to be the better land. The text says that *"Lot looked up and saw that the plain of the Jordan was well watered . . . like the land of Egypt." (v.10)* His heart was centered on wealth and the prospect of a better life. In his eyes, the valley looked like the Nile valley of Egypt that he had left behind. It was fertile and near the cities of the plain where he might experience some of the pleasures that he had left behind in Egypt. Abraham had moved Lot out of Egypt but could not take the Egypt out of Lot. Lot would move near Sodom and later move into Sodom. He seized what he wanted and saw it as the better choice, but it was a choice that would later destroy him.

Abram thinks of the family, but Lot thinks of himself. When anyone thinks like Lot, it leaves everyone broken. Lawsuits are threatened, and relationships are damaged for a long time. The miracle of our Lord is that it takes just one person, like Abram, to live humbly and diffuse the situation. Such humility comes as we trust the Lord to take care of us and do not try to gain the upper hand for ourselves. Such humility builds family relationships that money can't buy. Such trust also gives the Lord a chance to direct our future. As Lot made his choices, he began down the path of destruction. As Abram left the choice up to God, he continued on a path of blessing.

What if we change the future of that family fighting over their parent's inheritance? Instead of fighting, a few members of the family are willing to give others a choice and take whatever is left. All of the members of the family would get some of what they wanted, but the Lord could direct events so that each person got what they really needed. The family would have greater wealth because little would be lost to lawsuits. Family unity would be preserved, and the others would be amazed at the love shown by this Christian family. God would be honored, and the family would be stronger. Godly humility can change the future.

- Who have you quarreled with recently? If you could ask God to change one thing in that relationship, what would it be?

5. Choosing God
Genesis 13: 11-18

Context: The return from Egypt causes pain as the two flocks compete for the available choice pasture. Each man shows their character and values in the choices that they make. When Lot leaves, God reaffirms His promises.

Hustle, Hustle, Hustle! It is the chant of the football coach and the chant of our society. Run faster. Work harder. Grab all that you can as if your success depends on it. It is all about your choices and your effort. Don't be content with your situation, work harder and get more. Yet, where is God in all of this? Is God only about rewarding our efforts to work harder, faster and smarter? Often it would seem that God's role in our lives is to bless our efforts or provide the opportunities that will help us thrive. We pray fervently for God to make our plans successful. Yet, what if our plans are not what is really best for us? Do we want God to bless those plans or to give us a future that will bring blessings?

The old man was foolish enough to give him a choice *"So Lot chose for himself the whole plain of the Jordan."(v.11)* Lot saw the plains and grabbed them. In his mind this was the best choice and would give his animals an advantage. He never is mentioned building an altar or praying to the Lord. He knew what he wanted and probably thought that the opportunity meant that God was blessing him. Surely, he knew the reputation of the people that lived there (v.13), but it didn't matter to him. His plans would cause him a lot of heartache. His relationship with the people of the valley would cause his capture (Gen. 14). Later, the choice of Sodom would result in the loss of all his property and some of his family (Gen. 19), but he did not see that yet. He saw what he thought was the best and he wanted it. Like many today, he would make his own success.

I believe that Abram relies on his Lord and not his senses. Lot has chosen what he thought was the better land, but the Lord comes to Abram after Lot's departure to reaffirm His promise that the land all will belong to Abram and his descendants. God recommits to his promise *"All the land that you see I will give to you." (v.15)* As the months and years unfold, the relationship that Abram has with the Lord will outweigh all the hustle that Lot has shown in this bargain. Yes, Abram will have to wait for the land because the time is not yet ripe. Yet, Abram shows great contentment with the choice. He will live wherever the Lord places him and trust the Lord to make this land bring blessings.

God also reaffirms the promise for a multitude of descendants. *"I will make your offspring like the dust of the earth." (v.16)* Lot has departed for the valley and Abram is now alone. Does Abram have a sense that the two of them will never be as close as they once were? We will never know. Yet, even as his only relative in Palestine leaves, God reaffirms the promise of an heir. The land that stretches out in all directions will be filled with descendants from Abram. They will be as numerous as the dust of the earth. God will give him offspring who will own and fill the land. Having trusted in the Lord, Abram sees that his trust has not been misplaced. His greatest inheritance is the relationship he has with God.

Abram shows us the value of being content with God's choices for our lives. Often, we wear ourselves out by trying to control things that are beyond our ability. The hustle and bustle of the world often doesn't lead to lasting results. We press for the corner office, the most talented children, or for the bargain of the year. We often end up with something glamorous like Lot's choice that will become a disaster in the future. Abram's humble choice to let Lot choose and be content with the Lord's portion is a model for us. God knows the future and we don't. Let us ask for His direction and be happy with the share that we have from Him. His choice will always be better than we could have made for ourselves.

To live like Abram is to be the best employee, parent and friend as we live humbly and lovingly with others. Someone else may get that corner office, but they will have its pressures. Someone else's child may be the greatest athlete in the school until someone else surpasses them. Others may seem to thrive with hustle, but they often do so at a cost to their health, their friendships and their future. Those who humbly live in God's blessings will not regret it. He has the path that leads to real success. Let us humbly serve the Lord and build relationships with God and others.

- What are you dissatisfied with in your life right now?

  How has that dissatisfaction affected you?

6. Who Controls Your Fate?
Gen. 14:1-13

Context: This text records the first war mentioned in the Bible. Eastern kings led by Shinar (modern day Iraq) attack the southern kings (including Sodom and Gomorrah) over the wealth of trade routes between Mesopotamia and Egypt. Sadly, Lot ends up in the middle of the battle.

Your friends determine your fate. If you don't believe it, look at your kids. The friends that your children choose determine their future. Let a child get in with the wrong group and you will have nothing but trouble. Friends influence children to alcohol, drugs and a host of other destructive habits. Let a child make friends in a good sports or music program where they are around well-behaved children and they often stay out of trouble. It really is no different for adults. Adults who frequent the bars or hang around with people who have trouble holding down a job will be pulled down by their friends. Adults who spend a lot of time around strong Christians or have a set of friends with strong morals will be pulled up by these friends. Who you spend your life with will determine your fate.

This is the first battle mentioned in the Bible. Its importance is its strong connection to Abram and Lot. The five cities of the plains rebel against their masters, the four cities of the east. The armies from the east march out to wage war on the rebellious cities of the plains. In response, *"the king of Sodom . . . marched out and drew up their battle lines." (v.8)* One would have expected that the five cities could defend themselves on their own turf, but they are routed and many fall into tar pits in the midst of their escape. The conquering army takes the goods and food of Sodom and Gomorrah as they depart. Such bounty was used to pay for and feed their troops. This is where this battle connects with the characters of the Bible.

Lot had moved from outside the city (13:12) to moving into the city (14:12). Now he would share their fate. Nothing in the text says that he went out into the battle, but *"They also carried off Abram's nephew Lot and his possessions." (v.12)* He would pay the price for their loss because he had now become one of them. Perhaps, he felt that he could separate himself from their evil and live among them, but not really become one of them. Whatever his thoughts, he had thrown his portion in with Sodom and now was reaping the fruit of his choices. The capture of Lot demonstrates that you will share the fate of those who you call friends.

At first, while the battle is raging in the valley below, Abram is living safely up in the hills of Palestine. *"Now Abram was living near the great trees of Mamre the Amorite."(v.13)* The battle never threatens his flocks or his people. Having never allied himself with the people of Sodom, he and his people were safe up on the hill and were unaffected by the battle below. He had cast his portion with the Lord. He had avoided the lure of the evil cities. He had made alliances with some of the Amorites (14:13) for protection and trade but had remained true to his God. Lot had desired the riches and the lifestyle of the world. Abram was content to live with his Lord.

Who do you associate with? No one can enter the house of the worldly and not be untouched. Their fate will affect your work, your family and your life. They may lure you in with their riches or excitement, but you will also share in their destiny.

We cannot expect God to protect us from harm when we try to live in the wild animal's den. Abram was not isolated, but he did live apart from those who lived caustic lives in the valley below. We should try to help our neighbor, but we dare not live among them lest we become one of them. As we choose our friends and associates, we often choose our future. Those who cast their lot with the world will face the consequences that Lot faced.

One doubts that this story would have even been mentioned in scripture if Lot had lived with his flocks in the valley rather than in the city. The armies might have looted the city and not even known that Lot and his flocks were three or four miles away. The danger might have all passed him by as he lived outside the city and not in the middle of Sodom. We do have a choice. We can live safely in the hills with God or dare to live in the midst of evil. We all know people who have gotten into the wrong crowd and feel that life would be different if they had a different set of friends. As you think of your own life, consider how it would be blessed if you sought out Godly friends who could nurture you and help you draw closer to the Lord. Our friends do have an effect on our fate.

Godly friends lift us up and worldly friends can pull us down.

- Which of your friends tend to bring out the best in you?
  How could you develop those relationships so that they lift
  you even higher?

7. Rescuing Others in Trouble
Gen. 14:13-24

Context: Hearing that Lot has been taken, Abram does the unthinkable and wages ware on five kings with his 318 trained men. The result shows what God can do when we trust Him. It is a victory which Abram knows belongs only to the Lord.

Problems crash into our lives on a regular basis. Sometimes the problem is from our own mistakes. Sometimes trials come from just living in a sinful world. Abram has to deal with a problem that comes directly from the choices that his nephew Lot has made. Up in the hills, Abram could only watch as his nephew moved from the hills to the valley and into the city of Sodom. No doubt he had warned his nephew of the dangers of that evil city, but Lot had not listened. Now Lot was facing the consequences of his actions. In the same situation, it would be tempting to ignore someone we know who has made bad choices. Abram feels compelled to help and to put his own life on the line to save his nephew.

He acts because of compassion. *"When Abram heard that his relative had been taken captive, he called out the 318 trained men born in his household and went in pursuit as far as Dan".(v.14)* News came to Abram that his nephew had been captured and was being taken by the four kings of the east as bounty. Compassion welled up in him and he felt that he had to rescue his wayward nephew. Abram had stayed away from the battle because he was an outsider. He was separate from the politics and intrigue of the world around him. Yet, now that Lot's life was on the line, he felt compelled to act even though Lot had acted foolishly. He was willing to do something to help his nephew and others overcome the danger that they now found themselves in. He was separated from the world, but that didn't mean that he was uncaring or indifferent.

After Abram wins the battle, he acknowledges the source of the victory. *"And blessed be God Most High, who delivered your enemies into your hand." Then Abram gave him a tenth of everything." (v.20)* Little is known about Melchizedek, but the text says that he was a priest of God. Together they celebrate with a meal what the Lord has accomplished. Abram acknowledges that the victory belongs to the Lord. He gives the first tithe to the Lord off the top. Such celebration kept Abram from boasting about what he and his small band of men had done. It helped him from being defeated by Satan after this victory or from falling into fear like Elijah did after the victory at Mt. Carmel. God had brought total victory, and this was a celebration and worship of the Lord for all that He had done.

In contrast to Melchizedek, Abram will have little to do with the king of Sodom. *"That I will accept nothing belonging to you, not even a thread or the thong of a sandal, so that you will never be able to say, 'I made Abram rich."* (v.23) To many, Abram had earned the spoils of war that were being offered to him. He had conquered the foreign kings and deserved the goods that were now before him. Yet, Abram would not be lured by the riches. He did not want to be connected with the king of Sodom or with any of the fruits of this battle. He did not want evil men to claim that they had been a part in his success. Lot had been rescued and the Lord had been acknowledged. He asks for a share to the leaders that have gone with him, yet he will take nothing from the king of Sodom since he does not want to be tempted. He avoids trouble by spurning an allegiance or connection with evil.

There are times when compassion requires that we act. We see the pain and suffering of others and the love of the Lord moves us to do something to help. It may require a sacrifice or may put us in danger, but we know that the Lord would want us to reach out to help. Our Lord wants us to show His love to a troubled world. Yet, such action also brings spiritual dangers. It means that we may have to go into worlds that we have avoided because of their evil. We need to keep our distance from the evil and celebrate any victories that come at the hand of the Lord. We act on His behalf in love and expect Him to guide us. We do well to remember that victories belong to Him.

The challenge is always to help, but not get caught up in the evil that is destroying someone we love. As Christians we want to avoid the two extremes. We don't want to be uncaring and ignore another's need. That would be to ignore our responsibility to others. Yet, we don't want to give in to evil and lose the character that God gave us. Honor the Lord and rely on His power while making no alliance with evil. It is hard to do, but it is the way of victory for the day and for life.

- Who have you helped recently? How did you show the character of God as you helped someone in need?

8. Fear Can Follow Success
Gen. 15:1-6

Context: Abram's victory was total, but he fears that the eastern kings will return and attack him in retaliation. God responds with a display of encouragement to allay the fears of His beloved patriarch and point to a rich future.

We used to call it "waiting for the other shoe to drop". Things were going so well that we were just waiting for something bad to happen. We were afraid that disaster was just around the corner after such a great success. While it is unwise to trust your emotions, we must admit that we are all emotional people and that we can't fully suppress our emotions. Many of the biblical characters like David in the Psalms or Jeremiah in his prophecy shared honestly with God how they felt. It is a relief to know that God does not reject us when our emotions go wild. God comes to Abram and to us in order to help His people and teach them to trust Him when fear follows triumph.

The battle was over and everyone was home safe, yet fear gripped the man of God. At first, he had stayed out of the battle and the affairs of the kings. The capture of Lot had changed everything and put him at the center of their war. Would the four kings now regroup and seek retribution? His heart was torn with fear and so God came to comfort him. The armies that he defeated were big, but God is bigger. *"Don't be afraid, Abram. I am your shield"* (v.1) was God's comfort. The world around you is big and dangerous, Abram, but you can trust your God to protect you. God would defeat the enemies of the Jews for centuries. God can be depended upon in every situation.

As Lot went back to Sodom, it became apparent that Lot would never be the heir that God had promised. Abram confesses to the Lord his second fear *"I remain childless"* *(v.2).* Abram was getting old and the child had not yet come. How would the promises be fulfilled? How would his descendants inherit this land or make him a blessing to the whole world if there was not even a single son. In an act of love, God does not rebuke His servant. He simply reminds Abram that the promise is still intact. His descendants would be as numerous as the stars. We know that to be true, but

Abram had to believe the word of his God. His faith in those words is the foundation of his relationship with the Lord. He must learn that God's promises will be fulfilled in God's time and way. The believer is to have faith in God so that he is accessible when God chooses to make the impossible happen.

The battle had shown him how easily land could be gained or lost. He echoes a third fear,*" How can I know that I will gain possession of it (the land)?" (v.8)* The five kings of the valley could not hold the land against the four kings of the east. How could he know that his descendants would gain the land that was not theirs at the present and hold onto it? God comforts His servant by renewing the promise that the land would belong to Abram and his people. Oddly, Abram never saw that day, but his descendants to this day own the land. Others have taken it over the centuries, but God continues to honor the promise He made to Abram and return the land to his descendants.

What is the key to defeating Satan when he wants failure to follow success? *"Abram believed the Lord and he credited it to him as righteousness." (v.6)* Open yourself up to the Lord as Abram did and believe the promises that God has made to you in His word. We are not saved by making promises to God, but by believing the promises that He has made to us. The fears that we face are natural and it is not surprising that we face them. Faith defeats them and trusts God to handle the "what if's" that everyone faces. Such faith is a gift from God as He comforts His people. The victorious know that the promises of God in scripture are always true. Fear will wilt when the word of God powerfully lifts up God's people.

How would life change if your fears changed to faith? You would spend less time worrying after a great success about what could go wrong. The joy of the Lord is stronger than the worries of the evil one. Like Abram, our weapon against worry is to listen to God. When the fears have you frozen, the word of God can thaw you out. Read your Bible and let your loving God speak to your fears. Pray about them like Nehemiah, David or others have done so that your Lord can comfort you and push Satan's worries away. It is natural to fear. It is harder to have faith. Yet, faith will overcome fear so that joy and success in life and ministry can be ours.

- What are you worrying about right now? What help could

  seek from God for those worries?

9. God Has Our Back
Gen. 15:8-19

Context: Having repeated the promises of chapter 12, God now demonstrates that He is in control of the future with a rare revelation of the future to Abram. Abram's descendants will receive what God has promised, but it will not always be easy.

There are times that I worry in spite of my faith in God. I know God has things covered. The world may threaten me, and life may seem to fall apart, but it is the Lord who rules the future. Every Christian knows that and believes it, but questions remain. Our emotions are often still afraid and even leave us shaken in the face of trials. How do we resolve this dilemma? I find that I have to resolve it on my knees in prayer. I have to throw myself on the mercy of God so that He may calm my fears. I need courage to act on what I believe and not what I feel. It may surprise you to learn that even Abram wrestled as we often do. Yet, it was in this moment that Abram learned that God had his back and ours.

Abram learns that the Lord controls the future. Abram is concerned whether his descendants can gain control of the land and enjoy it. God does not hide the difficulties that the people of Israel will face. They will spend 400 years in a land that is not their own. Yet, God will not forget them. God promises *"I will punish the nation they serve as slaves and afterward they will come out with great possessions."(v.14)* God will bring them back to this land and will give it to them at the proper time. Why will God wait so long? God tells us in verse 16 that he is long suffering and will delay the judgment on the people of this land so that they might have more time to repent. God in His mercy will give the land to Israel at just the right time.

God gives to Abram a unique sign to show that the promise is true. *"When the sun had set, and darkness had fallen, a smoking firepot with a blazing torch appeared and passed between the pieces." (v.17)* In ancient times, the cutting of a covenant was a ritual that bound two parties in a promise. The animals were cut in half and the two parties would walk together through the divided animals as a sign that if either of them broke the covenant that they be cut in two like these animals. For this covenant, only God walked between the animals. The promise of deliverance for Abram's descendants and their inheritance of the land did not depend on Abram. God would bring it to pass unconditionally. This was a covenant of grace. Abram did not have to worry whether his descendants would sin and lose the promise of the land. The promise did not depend on them; it was all up to God.

How big was the promise? *"To your descendants I give this land from the river of Egypt to the great river, the Euphrates"* *(v.18)* Lest Abram think that the land of the covenant was an only a small section, God elaborated on how big the promise really was. God was all powerful and the promise that He was making encompassed a vast region. Such a promise was possible because God is almighty. David and Solomon would exercise control over a vast area and rule it for the people of Israel. Jesus Christ would rule over an even larger kingdom than the one God elaborates here. God is not bound by our weakness. Nothing is impossible for Him.

When our heart is troubled, like Abram's was, we need to come and see the greatness of our God. Our God is the God of history and all the future is under His control. We worry about our future and the future of our children. We need to place them in God's hands. He is the almighty one who will care for His people. He is the gracious one who gives us better than we deserve. When we place our future in His hands, His plans for us are infinitely greater than we could imagine. He has no limits. There is nothing that He cannot do.

Abram's question was not a sign of unbelief. It was a prayer for assurance. Our heads and hearts battle all the time in the arena of faith. There is no reason to fight that battle alone when we have the power of prayer. The peace that we can have when the Lord comes and answers our fears is priceless. His word shows us that He is in control of the future. His touch when we are on our knees calms the fears that we face with the power of His grace and presence. Why live in fear when we can have His comfort? Why wrestle with doubt alone when we can let our Lord wrestle at our side. Those who know the greatness of their God will slay the dragon of fear with the sword of faith.

- What are you afraid of right now? What sign would remind

  you that the Lord has your future in His hands?

10. Waiting For Heaven
Genesis 16: 1-4

Context: Ten years have passed since the promises of chapter 12 and yet there still is no child for Abram and Sarai. The couple decides to take matters into their own hands. They hatch a plan to provide the heir for God, but they cause themselves a lot of heartache instead.

Waiting can be one of the hardest things that we have to do as a Christian. We keep witnessing to a neighbor and see little results. A young couple waits for a baby that doesn't seem to come. We send in dozens of resumes and no job seems to appear when we are out of work. We believe that the Lord has a plan for us, but it is hard to see an unseen God at work. It is hard to wait for a God who thinks in centuries when we think in hours or days. Our patience wanes and our trust can slip away. Soon we take matters into our own hands and hope that it all works out. Such is the problem for Abram and Sarai who have waited longer than they ever hoped for a child.

It has been ten years since Abram first came to Palestine. God had repeated the promise of a son to Abram on more than one occasion. Yet, at the age of 85, we are told *"Now Sarai, Abram's wife had borne him no children." (v.1)* How painful that must have been for both of them. The years for bearing children were fast slipping away. I picture Abram praying and pleading with God for the promise to be fulfilled. Yet, the time had not come. How much easier it had been to trust God ten years ago when the promise was new. Now, ten year later, there were doubts. Did God mean that he would have a physical son or was it all just an analogy to teach him some truth?

Sarai hatched a plan that would solve their dilemma. Up till now, the Bible does not record that God had promised that Sarai was to be the mother of the peoples as numerous as the stars. The promises were all to Abram. She makes the sacrifice and takes *'her Egyptian maid servant Hagar and gave her to her husband to be his wife." (v.3)*. Hagar would bear the child that would fulfill the promises. All the promises that God had made to Abram could now come true. This child would inherit the land and would make Abram's name great. At first, her motives seem noble. She will step aside in order that her husband may have his heir. Sadly, solutions that do not include God are often a formula for disaster.

Her plan has unintended consequences. The maid who has now become the second wife has an attitude. *"When she knew she was pregnant, she began to despise her mistress." (v.4)* As the mother of the heir, Hagar felt like she deserved special treatment. She, not Sarai, would be the mistress of the household. Sarai, however, would not tolerate such feelings and pushed back. She was not about to be second rate behind an Egyptian slave. She blamed her husband for the problem and wanted him to make things right. When he refuses to act, she begins to mistreat her servant. The perfect plan unravels and causes a lot of pain and suffering for all those involved. God did know what was best after all.

Patience and trust are interlocked. When we wait patiently for a plane that is overdue, we trust that the airline will still get us where we want to go. Our struggle in life comes when we don't believe that God is still at work on our behalf. We are waiting "at the gate" so to speak and the answer doesn't seem to be coming. We think that God has forgotten us and we are on our own. Like a traveler calling other carriers to see if they can book a different flight, we try to solve our problems rather than wait for God. The results can be just as disastrous for us as they were for Abram. If we want to avoid those disasters, we have to trust the Lord. We must begin to think about the many times that the Lord has helped us in the past. We need to do things that open opportunities for the Lord to help us. Success comes when we trust God rather than taking matters in our own hands.

Sadly, the pain has just begun for Abram. The household will be the place of an uneasy truce for years with bitterness as a constant companion. Abram will grow fond of his son Ishmael during the next fifteen years only to have to send him away. Ishmael and Isaac will not be able to get along and it will be Isaac, the son of promise, which can remain. (Gen. 21:14). The children of Ishmael and Isaac will be enemies through the years. This bitterness was not part of God's plan. How different things would have been for Abram and Sarai during those years if they had been patient with God's plans. As you think of short-circuiting God's plans because they don't come soon enough, ask yourself what heartache you are creating for yourself in the years to come. Waiting for heaven may not be easy, but God always has a plan for us and He will not forget us or His promises.

- As you look back on your life and ministry, when have you been tempted to make God promises happen faster? What was the result?

11. Submit to the Lord and Have Peace Genesis 16: 4-16

Context: Abram is 86 years old when Hagar bears Ishmael as his first son. The birth brings misery to the family. God must bring peace and order to the troubled family. Abram's household cannot have two wives.

Wars and political battles litter the evening news. Anger and jealousy invade the relationships that we have with family and friends. Too often people try to solve their problems by destroying someone else. Why can't people get along? Why must we cause suffering upon each other as we try to relieve the pain that each of us is feeling? The simple answer is often that we don't trust God. We don't trust God to protect us and to care for our future and so we fall into solutions that pit each of us against one another. Abram and Sarai had not asked God for His solution on the unfulfilled promise of an heir. The committee of two worked out their answer and found that it caused problems instead of giving joy. As we will see, each person in this triangle contributed to make things worse.

As soon as Hagar knew she was pregnant, *"She began to*

despise her mistress." (v.4) You can easily imagine the Egyptian handmaiden thinking that she was now the woman of the house. Sarai would be tormented by her new rival like Hannah, the mother of Samuel many years later (1 Samuel 1). Hagar believed that she was the mother of Abram's heir and had a status that Sarai had failed to achieve. If she had maintained the position of a servant, things might have been different. Yet her pride caused her to want to throw off her lowly position and challenge her mistress.

Sarai values her status as the woman of the house and may feel guilty that she has not been able to produce the heir that Abram wants. She takes out her anger and frustration on both her husband and the maidservant. She confronts her husband. 'You are responsible for the wrong I am suffering." (v.5) While she was the one who came up with the scheme to produce an heir, she now blames Abram for the whole problem. He should have seen this problem coming. He should have made sure that she was respected the way that she deserved. Instead of working together and presenting a unified front, she attacks her husband and then attacks the arrogant maid.

Even Abram does not deal well with the conflict. He shirks his duty and gives the problem right back to Sarai. *"Your servant is in your hands, do with her whatever you think best."* *(v.6)* The servant is hers and as mistress of the household, Sarai should be able to deal with her servants. He fails his wife. He fails his child that Hagar is carrying. He even fails to act as the master of the house and settle a dispute in his family. The conflict grows as each person in this trio looks only to their own interests.

The Lord sees the misery of this family and steps in. The angel of the Lord tells Hagar. *"Go back to your mistress and submit to her." (v.9)* She cannot run from the problem that she helped create. Because of His love for Abram and for the child, God promises that the child will have *"descendants too numerous to count." (v.10)* God's intervention brings some peace to the family. Hagar returns, and her story must have convinced both Sarai and Abram to live in peace as well. God's intervention reminds us that God is concerned with our pain, even when it is self-inflicted. As we listen to Him, peace can come.

The key to peace is submission. Like Hagar, we need to submit to the Lord and live with God's character instead of selfish pride. Like Sarai, we need to work with others instead of blaming others for our problems. Like Abram, we need to submit to the Lord and lead others to solutions instead of ignoring problems. It is only when members of a family submit to the Lord and trust the Lord with the future that a family can overcome the issues that Satan wants to use to separate us. If we live and love as God's people, we can have the blessings of God's people.

The world constantly tells us to assert our rights, but God calls us to have His character and to live humbly. The child was not in God's plan, but the Lord would not abandon the household or its members. Sadly, the tentative peace that this family achieved would not last forever. The birth of Isaac (Gen. 21) would reunite the struggle between the women and between their sons. Ishmael would be forced to leave for good. Submission was not easy for this man who *'will live in hostility toward all his brothers." (v.12)* When we don't submit and love others as God's people, there is always a

consequence.

- Who are you feeling at odds with right now? What issue

  between you could you give to the Lord?

12. A great God deserves great people
Genesis 17: 1-14

Context: God renews His covenant thirteen years after the birth of Ishmael with five "I will" statements. The time is coming for Isaac to be born and God commands circumcision as a sign of His covenant with Abraham.

There can be no doubt that we have an Almighty God. Yet, our world often doesn't see Him that way. They see His church and it seems to them lifeless and empty. They see churches that are filled with entertainment value and not powerful preaching. They see Christians who live no differently than their non-Christian friends and coworkers. Is it any wonder that people think that our God is weak and powerless because of what they see among His people? A great God will be shown to the world by great people. When His people reflect His values and His actions, the world notices and sees that our God is truly great.

God reveals Himself to us as the one who is all sufficient and calls His children to show His greatness to the world. *"I am the Lord Almighty, walk before me and be blameless."*

(v.1) Thirteen years before this, Abram and Sarai had tried to make God's promises come true by their own hand. They had devised a plan where Abram would take Hagar as his concubine and give birth to Ishmael. The plan had caused them nothing but grief for it was not God's plan. God calls them to live as His people and trust Him. He wants them to follow Him and live in His promise. The time for the promise to be fulfilled was close. The time had come for God to show the world through Abram and Sarai exactly how great He really was.

God begins the revelation by reaffirming the promises made almost twenty-five years before. *"As for me, this is my covenant with you. You will be the father of many nations."* *(v.4)* Abram may have begun to give up on ever seeing the promises come true, but God had not forgotten them. God reaffirms the promise of a great host of descendants. He reaffirms the promise that Abram will change the world through his descendants. He reaffirms the promise that the land will belong to those descendants as well. All those promises are affirmed and are based not on something that

Abram will do. Each begins with "I will" to show that the promises are based solely on the power of the Almighty God. Nothing that Abram or his descendants can do will change those promises. God has spoken. It will happen.

The promise of land was based solely on the grace and love of God. Yet, Abraham and the Jews would enjoy the land only if they were faithful to the Lord. *"As for you, you must keep my covenant, you and your descendants after you for the generations to come." (v.9)* Circumcision was to be a sign that the people of Israel belonged to the Lord and were willing to walk with the Lord. They would enjoy the land, as in the days of David, when they were faithful to the Lord. They would find life hard when the people and their kings forgot God and worshipped idols. A great God deserved a people willing to worship Him and show Him to the world. If they did this, they would enjoy the blessings that God had in store for them as His people.

God is still great. He is still the Lord of the universe who powerfully runs the world. He is the savior of all mankind who listens to the prayers of His people. Many don't think of God that way, however. They see Him poorly because of the way that His people act in their daily lives. Jews in the Old Testament and Christians today are to live differently than the world around them. They are to be a people of character and loving kindness in an immoral and selfish world. They are to be a people that reflect their great God so that the world can see Him as He really is. When God's people forget God and become like the world, the world does not see the real God. They see someone who is no different than the world and not worth their worship or adoration.

A great God deserves great people. Most of us can think of at least one Christian whose faith shined with character and love. These were people who reflected God. We admired them and wanted to be like them. What would your world be like if the majority of Christians you knew lived with values, character and love? How would that impact the level of joy in the church, in their families and in their communities? How would it change the world's view of God? Abraham is beloved in his day and in ours because he shows the character of the Lord. As you and I walk with the Lord and live with His character, we can show Him to the world and let them see why we believe in and love our God. We can let our world know just how great our God really is.

- What is one thing that you can do today or this week to strengthen your walk with the Lord?

13. When God calls us to something new
Genesis 17: 15-27

Context: Abraham is 99 years old when God reaffirms the covenant. Sarah is renamed for she, not Hagar, will bear the son of promise. In doing so, God makes it clear that Ishmael is not the son of God's covenant promises.

New isn't always better. I still use an older version of Word to write my devotions. I know that the newer versions can do things that this version cannot do. I just hate the idea of learning new commands and buttons. I imagine that you have something that you just don't want to give up. It may simply be an old T-shirt that reminds you of good days in your past. It might be an old car that works perfectly fine. Yet, what if the thing that you want to hold onto is something that God wants you to give up? What if you want to hold onto a grudge that you have with a coworker? What if you are unwilling to give up cursing or flirting with someone at work? What if what you or I don't want to give up is something that is getting in the way of our relationship with the Lord? If that is the case, God may be calling you to something new.

Such is the case in the text for Abraham. Abraham had come to love his son Ishmael. Here, he pleads *"If only Ishmael might live under your blessing!" (v.18)* He had watched the young man grow for 13 years. Ishmael was his own flesh and blood whom he loved dearly. God had promised that Abraham would have an heir through which God would bless the world. Couldn't God make Ishmael the seed of that promise? Couldn't God give His blessing upon Ishmael so that through him all the nations of the earth would be blessed? Abraham had come to understand God's promise that Sarah was to be the mother of all nations (v.15). If that was true, then Ishmael was not part of God's plan. Abraham worried what would become of the son that he loved.

While Ishmael would not be the son of promise, God would still bless him. God says, *"And as for Ishmael, I have heard you; I will surely bless him." (v.20)* Ishmael was not the son God had promised, but our God of love would bless Ishmael for Abraham's sake. Ishmael would be a great nation in his own right and bear twelve sons. He could not take the place of Isaac, but God would keep the promises that He had already made concerning the boy (Gen 16:10-12). God also knew what Abraham would soon find out (Gen 21:8f), namely that the two sons could not exist side by side. Ishmael brought dissension into the house, but Isaac would bring laughter. Ishmael was a human plan while Isaac was of the plan of God. Ishmael could not be the seed that God was talking about, but God would bless him.

Isaac would begin the new era. *"But my covenant I will establish with Isaac whom Sarah will bear to you by this time next year." (v.21)* Abram, the man who tried to work things out for himself, would now become Abraham, the patriarch and friend of God. The time of the promise had come. In the past, Abram took things into his own hands. Now Abraham would trust the Lord with his future. God declares that 99-year-old Abraham was ready to become the father of a multitude and live in the promise that God had given him. Ishmael represented the past while Isaac was the future. In the miracle of Isaac's birth, God would show that all the other promises that He had made to Abraham would come true as well. As hard as it would be, Abraham needed to let go of the past and look ahead to God's future for him and for his descendants in Isaac.

Change is not always easy for us. It is seldom easy to move, to take a new job, or to point our lives in a new direction. Sometimes, God calls us to do just that. We need to listen to God's direction for our lives instead of trying to get Him to bless the direction that we think that we want to go. We cannot attempt to control our world and make the good promises of God come into our lives. Our desires need to give way to what the Lord has in mind for us. We may love the old ways, but God may have something new and better for us. We need to be willing to let go of the comfortable and step out in faith when God calls our name.

God often calls us to get out of His way as He makes a new future for us. He calls us to embrace big dreams that we may think are impossible. He calls us to trust Him even when we want to take the safe and easy way. Abraham would eventually send Ishmael away (Gen. 21:14) because the old and the new cannot exist together. We may be able to keep the old T-shirt because it reminds us of things we love, but we need to follow if the Lord calls us in a new direction. God wants us to have the best and sometimes that means we have to let go of the old to have His new.

- If God called you to make a major change in your life, what is one thing that you would find hard to give up? How might that thing be holding you back?

14. Christian hospitality
Genesis 18: 1-8

Context: A short time after the events of chapter 17, God appears in human form. God appears in human form to reaffirm the covenant and to share with Abraham a message about Sodom.

Hospitality is a dying art. Hospitality requires that a person break out of an isolated and self-sufficient life to care for another person. Busy lives make it hard to notice others or to care. Air-conditioned fortresses keep us from connecting with our neighbors. Gone are the days when people sat out on the front lawn or stairs and shared a lemonade with those who passed by. Now, we would think it strange if a neighbor came to our door just wanting to chat. We would be irritated if an acquaintance called us at 2 AM with a desperate need. Yet, the act of kindness to a neighbor in need is powerful. It shows the love and mercy of Jesus in a special way. Abraham has become a kind man. He is a model of what hospitality looks like.

The first thing we notice is that Abraham gives help to

others immediately. *"When he saw them, he hurried from the entrance of his tent to meet them and bowed low to the ground." (v.2)* He could have pretended that he was asleep, or he could have asked them to wait while he finished some other important task. Instead, Abraham gets up right away and takes care of their needs as quick as humanly possible. He does not wait till the day gets cooler or ignore them for a while to see if they will go away. He finds the best food that he has and serves it to them in a timely manner. He assumes that the travelers are hungry and urges Sarah and his servant to prepare the food quickly. He stands under a tree nearby as they eat ready to help them with any other need that they have. He will not make them wait.

The second thing about hospitality is that Abraham served them personally. *"Let me get you something to eat so that you can be refreshed and then go on your way." (v.5)* Although he is ninety-nine years old and has over a 300 servants (Gen. 14:4), he does not hand off their care to someone else. During the heat of the day, Abraham will personally see to their needs. He manages every detail of their meal. He supervises the choice of the calf and calls for Sarah to prepare fresh bread for the strangers. He stands by ready and waiting to personally take care of them as they eat their meal. His hospitality has a personal touch that seeks to make sure that everything is just right.

Finally, Abraham is generous to his guests. The meal is not just a few morsels that were left over from a previous meal. *"He then brought some curds and milk and the calf that had been prepared and set these before them." (v.8).* The meal was a choice calf and side dishes that made this a banquet fit for royalty. It was a thoughtful gift to the travelers with no mention of anything that Abraham expected in return. His generosity was genuine, and he gave them the best that he had. The guests were important to Abraham and he showed it with bread of fine flour (v.6) and a choice tender calf (v.7). He is a model for those who see the needs of others and share what the Lord has given with them with a big heart.

Christian hospitality is a great witness that gives glory to God. People watch our kindness or lack of kindness to others. Our children notice when we are kind to the next-door neighbor, a family member or even the beggar we meet on the street. When Christians show hospitality, people see the love and care of our God. A coworker notices if we are willing to give them our time when they need help with a difficult project or with a problem at home. People notice when we treat others with a smile and lend a helping hand. Such acts of generosity support our witness as we talk about our generous God. People see the kindness of Jesus through us and connect with Him by the love that we share.

We also notice the kindness of others when they help us. Someone who stops to help us when our car breaks down is an "angel". The neighbor who helps us when we are sick is a "gift from God'. Think of what the world would be if every Christian took time to help just one person who is in need every day. Acts of kindness would change the culture in our home, our workplace, our neighborhood. The love of Jesus is often infectious. Others may be encouraged by our hospitality to be kind to others. Hospitality changes the climate of our world and makes each of the places where we live a better place to be.

- What is your first thought when someone asks you for help at work or at home? How can you be more open to helping out someone in need?

15. Test time
Genesis 18: 1-15

Context: He has made the promises to Abraham, now it is time for Sarah to receive the promise of a child first hand. She laughs at the promise that she will be the mother of a nation despite having seen so many miracles.

At first, I was not sure that I wanted to trust a GPS for directions. Little by little, I have gained confidence in the directions that the GPS voice gives. Those directions often don't make sense, but I have learned to follow them anyway. Likewise, the Bible is filled with promises from God that are sometimes hard to believe. Fortunately, God is willing to teach us to trust Him. He will come to us and stretch our faith little by little in order to make it stronger. He will help us to trust the simple promises so that we may one day learn to trust the greater promises. God wants to teach us to trust Him in the little things so that we will trust Him when life gets tough and failure is not really an option.

The three men had come unannounced and had been treated kindly as travelers in a harsh land. When Abraham realizes that the visitor is the Lord is unclear. Yet, the visitor

makes a promise that Abraham had heard only from the Lord.

"I will surely return to you about this time next year, and Sarah

your wife will have a son." (v.10) It is clear that God has

something special to reaffirm to Sarah. Abraham had been

told earlier that Sarah would be Isaac's mother (Gen. 17:19),

but God wants Sarah to hear it first-hand. She will be given a

son by this time next year. The visitor's use of the name of

Sarah, a name that only God had given her, should have

tipped Abraham off that this was not an ordinary visitor. God

was revealing Himself and repeating the promise. God tests

Sarah to see if faith has taken hold in Sarah's life. Does she

trust the Lord to do what He has said He will do for her?

Sadly, Sarah laughs at the prospect of God's promise

coming true. *"After I am worn out and master is old, will I now*

have this pleasure?" (v.12) Her doubts rob her of the joy the

announcement should have brought. She fails God's test

because she looks at herself and not at God. Her body is frail

and old. By itself, she could not bear a child. Yet, if she looks

at God with faith, she will realize that God is a God who can do anything. The promise was not based on her ability, but on the power and ability of God. The birth of the child was to be a miracle that would show both Sarah and Abraham that God would keep all the promises that He had made. The birth of Isaac was to be a sign to the world about the power and ability of God to do all things.

God gets to the heart of the matter when He asks, *"Is anything too hard for the Lord?" (v.14).* Sarah had seen great miracles. She had seen this God bring a plague on an Egyptian pharaoh in order to save her from her husband's foolishness. She had seen how the Lord had defeated the mighty armies that had threatened Sodom and Lot. God's power was evident and yet she found it hard to believe a promise God had continued making for 25 years. She had seen many miraculous things done by God, but this seemed too hard even for God. Sarah failed the test, but God would lovingly teach her that God's promises do come true. She would learn that a God who could bring the miracle birth of a son could keep all His promises, too. Nothing was too hard for our God.

There will be times when our very survival may depend on trusting God. It may be an illness like cancer. It may be a time when our job is lost, or a family member is hurting. In those times when life seems to be broken, God wants us to trust His promises in scripture and seek His answer to our problems. God knows that all of us will face those days some time in life. He doesn't want us to try to solve the crisis by ourselves, but to trust Him. For that reason, He will use opportunities and tests to teach us little by little to trust Him in every situation. He wants your faith to grow so you will expect your God to do the impossible in times of good and in times of trouble.

You and I will not pass each test that the Lord gives us. God doesn't make the tests easy. His tests, however, are not to humiliate us, but to help us grow just as this test would help Sarah. As you face His tests, do not be afraid. Be open to God's lessons and learn from God's gentle hand. Accept each test as a time to learn from our loving and gentle God. His goal is always to prepare us for the challenges that are still coming in life. His tests can transform us and make us strong. Just as He transformed Sarai into Sarah, He will transform you. Day by day, God will teach you to trust Him to do the impossible.

- When do you find it hard to trust the Lord? What is one lesson that you would like the Lord to teach you in the coming year?

16. Praying for good
Gen. 18: 16-37

Context: Abraham shows how his heart has grown. He has concern for his wicked neighbors. Rather than wishing them harm, he shows that he has the love of the Lord for others.

Anger makes us irrational. Somehow, we wish that we could wave our hand and evil would be gone. We have been hurt by evil and want it judged immediately. We pray that God might come and wipe evil off the face of the earth. The trouble is that such blanket destruction can destroy the good with the bad. Evil people are often loved by good people. The destruction of the evil ones may wipe out the innocent with the guilty. Judgment can destroy everything in one attack. Wouldn't it be better to pray that the innocent be saved? Shouldn't we pray that the Lord might turn the hearts of evil people so that they become righteous? When we see the big picture, we see the innocent as well as the guilty. We see things with a heart like God.

An evil people live in the valley below Abraham. God knows what He must do, but His deep relationship with

Abraham presents a quandary. *"Shall I hide from Abraham what I am about to do?" (v.17)* Abraham is one of the few in scripture who truly knew God and is known by God. God's question shows that He is concerned about the effect of this decision on Abraham. He loves Abraham and knows that the decision will affect His servant. He chooses not to hide what He is about to do from this special man but seeks to help Abraham understand how terrible the cities really are. Abraham's heart will break, just as God's does, when he understands that the destruction of these cities is inevitable. It is important to God that Abraham understands why a righteous God must bring justice to the cities.

Abraham, like God, is concerned about the righteous. *"Will you sweep away the righteous with the wicked?" (v.23)* Evil comes in many shades of black and gray. Is there no hope, Lord, for the redemption of some of the people? Abraham knows that judgment will wipe away any chance for these people to repent. It is not that he is unaware of the terrible nature of their sin. He has lived near this city long enough to know their evil and its effect on the people living around them.

The heart of Abraham, however, has been touched by God's mercy. He pleads with the Lord that the chance of repentance might not be taken away if there is a chance that even ten people might be saved.

Perhaps it was the thought that Lot and the people that were special to him were down in those cities below that made Abraham think about the innocent among the guilty. *"Will you really sweep it away and not spare the place for the sake of the fifty righteous people in it?" (v.24)* Perhaps Abraham had some dealings with people down in the valley as he sold sheep or as he rescued the cities so long ago. Yes, there was so much evil there, but Abraham had seen the faces of these people. He struggles to believe that all of them are evil. It is for those faces that he pleads that the innocent not be swept away with the guilty. It is for the innocent that Abraham begs God for justice. He asks the Lord of all to be just to those who are good.

How should we pray when we are faced with the evil of our world? We see the face of evil and our first instinct is to have it dealt with quickly. Yet, how does the Lord think about evil and justice? Those with the heart of God think about the innocent as well as the guilty. They realize the terrible price of destruction upon the good as well as the bad. Thankfully, our God is more patient and more just than we are. We often think that He works too slowly, but the reality is that He is not rash. He has the wisdom to know when and how to punish evil so that the good are spared as often as possible. Like Abraham, we need to pray for justice and not vengeance. We need to pray that people have a chance to repent as a way to conquer evil.

If God were to wipe evil off the face of the earth, He would wipe away all of us and many that we love. I am sure that there are people that I have hurt in my life who would gladly have had me destroyed. Fortunately, our God is a God of mercy seeking the repentance of people just like me. He reaches out to those who would follow Him just as He did for Lot. God would rather lead people to repentance and new life than destroy their lives for being evil. Our prayers should have God's heart for people and count on the Holy Spirit's power to change people with the word. Wiping away evil brings no more good into the world. Changing hearts from evil to

righteousness makes the world better as the worldly become

saints.

- What advantage would you have if God could turn your

  greatest enemy into a friend you could depend on? How

  could that person be an asset in your life?

17. Learning God's will
Gen 18:16-33

Context: The depth of God's relationship with Abraham is shown in God's desire to help Abraham understand how evil Sodom and Gomorrah have become. God uses dialog to teach Abraham that not even 10 righteous people live in this place.

What is the purpose of prayer? Sometimes, prayers degrade into God's "to do list". We come to the drive up window of prayer and place our order. Prayer can become a place where we tell God what our needs are and what He should do about it. Sadly, I know that I could never order my parents that way and I doubt that such orders work with a Heavenly Father, either. I have found that it is better just to tell the Lord my needs and ask for His solution. Prayer becomes part of a dialogue between God and me when paired with scripture. I don't want God to do my will since I often don't have a clue what is best. I want to give God my concerns and find out what His perfect and wise will is for my life and for others. I have come to learn that prayer is a place that I learn what God is doing, not order God to do what I want.

Having told Abraham that Isaac will be born within the next year, the Lord proceeds to tell Abraham that the time has come to deal with the evil of Sodom and Gomorrah. I picture Abraham being shocked by the news, yet he has the confidence to ask a question. *"Will you sweep away the righteous with the wicked?" (v.25)* Abraham may have been thinking of Lot who lived in Sodom or just thinking about what this news from the Lord meant. What is amazing is that he never shies from speaking the question on his mind. He knows that the Lord will not destroy him or get angry with him for an honest question. Abraham trusts the Lord and is confident that the Lord will listen and give him an honest answer.

Abraham bases his questions for God on the knowledge that God is just and merciful. *"Far be it from you to do such a thing--to kill the righteous with the wicked, treating the righteous and the wicked alike. Far be it from you! Will not the Judge of all the earth do, right?" (v.25)* He doesn't beg God to do anything. He doesn't claim that God can't destroy the city or claim that the city is not evil. He simply wants to understand why God is doing what He is doing. He wants to understand how bad things in Sodom are and what has led this merciful God to destroy the people that He created. Abraham knows that God always does the right thing. A shocked Abraham is trying to understand what God has planned.

As the exchange continues, Abraham knows that conversation with the Lord is a gift. He speaks to God with deep humility and with the knowledge that it is blessing to have a God who is patient and willing to listen. *"Then Abraham spoke up again: "Now that I have been so bold as to speak to the Lord, though I am nothing but dust and ashes,"* (v.27) Abraham knows that he is a man, but he has a burning need that only the Lord can help him with. Lot is down in Sodom and only the Lord can save him. As the exchange concludes, Abraham senses that the city may not even have 10 righteous people. In the conversation, God has shown Abraham how evil the cities are and why He must act.

I believe that the Lord initiated this whole conversation with Abraham as a means to teach His beloved patriarch. God revealed His plan and His reason for wanting Abraham to know (v.17-19). He could have destroyed the city without ever setting foot on earth, but He took time to teach. God teaches a lesson of mercy and justice to His servant. He let Abraham work through all the arguments and come to the realization that Sodom must be destroyed. God can and will do the same for us in our prayers. As we pray over days or weeks about an illness or a job, God often lets us work through the arguments until we know what His will is.

The Bible encourages us to pray without ceasing. Some have asked why God needs to be persuaded and why God will not help us on the first request. It is not God that needs to be persuaded, but us. Praying next to a loved one who is suffering, God needs to let us see that a gracious God may need to take them to be with Him in heaven. Praying for a job, God may need to help us to see that this is not a good opportunity for us. Extended prayer is not to persuade God, but rather a tool to teach us. There are many times in life where the purpose of prayer is to learn the "what" and "why" of God's will in our life. God does know what is best for us.

Those who know the character and wisdom of God will want His will for them and not their own.

- If you could ask God any question about your life or about the future, what would you ask? What makes that question so important to you?

18. Be careful what you wish for
Gen. 19:1-29

Context: Sitting at the gateway of the city, Lot sat in a place of prominence and influence. He had moved from living outside the city to becoming a leader of the city about to be destroyed.

Money doesn't buy happiness. We know that, but we still desire money and the things that it can buy. Too often the things that I want don't really bring me joy. All of us have had items that we wanted badly and were disappointed when the luster was gone. It could be the new car that yearned for until we were saddled with the years of payments. It could be the promotion that only brought long hours and a lot of headaches. At first, we felt so blessed to have these things that we longed for. We might have even lifted up a prayer of thanksgiving to God for His wonderful gift. Soon, we realized that the reality is not what we envisioned. Such can be the lures of this world used by Satan to defeat us. Be careful what you wish for. Sometimes our dreams can have unintended consequences.

Lot had been enamored with Sodom for years. He had

gladly chosen the valley as his portion when Abram offered it. It offered him some of the excitement and joy that he had left behind in Egypt. Not content to live near the city, he had moved into the city and even become an official in the city (v.1). Now as the destruction of the city is evident, he is hesitant to let go and has to be pulled out of the city. *"When he hesitated, the men grasped his hand." (v.16).* Surely, he saw what was coming. Surely, he knew that he could not keep what he had in Sodom. It didn't matter. He loved the city and longingly looked back at the city. One wonders if he would have stayed if the angels had let him. Lot was not alone in his attraction to the city. His wife had to take one last look (v.26) and it she lost her life.

Sadly, Lot had become one of the people of Sodom. He knows the danger of letting the two men stay in the square and urges them to come into the relative safety of his home. He fears what the people of his city would do to the strangers. It doesn't help. The town comes to Lot's door and demands that the men be brought to them. When confronted with the sexual advances of the men of the city on his guests, Lot does the unthinkable. He offers his daughters up to the mob. *"Look, I have two daughters who have never slept with a man." (v.8)* How far the morals of Lot have slipped! No sane man would consider giving his children away like that. A sane man would rather die. Having lived in the city for years, Lot has become one of them and is willing to sacrifice his children as a way out of a bad situation.

Having lived in the city and become one with it, Lot has lost his credibility. The messengers from God give Lot an opportunity to save others from the destruction. He rushes off to find the men who are to marry his daughters, but they refuse to believe him. *"His sons-in-law thought he was joking" (v.14)*. His wealth has grown in the city, but his influence has declined. His story of angels and coming destruction mean nothing coming from a man who has not talked about God or lived as one with faith in God. As he lost his morals and character, he lost the right to tell others what to do. They will not believe that he knows the best course of action.

In the end, Lot loses everything. His wealth and home are lost under the burning sulfur that rains on the city. His wife and future son in laws die having chosen Sodom rather than the opportunity to flee with Lot. His choice of Sodom has left him with very little. Such are the laments of the husband seeking advancement at work who forgets his family. Such are the laments of the person with a fancy house or car who is deep in debt because they never took time to make a budget. When we are not careful what we wish for, we may get dreams that turn into nightmares. In the short run, they may bring us a measure of happiness, but they will cause us unintended grief in the end. It is always wise to pray asking that the Lord would give us our wishes if they are what He knows are best. God's plan for us is always good.

Abram living up on the hill presents the opposite picture from Lot. He had waited on the Lord and the Lord had protected him. He had not been lured by the glitter of Sodom but had been content to live in the hills worshipping the Lord his God. Those who are content with what the Lord has for them will prosper. They will have things that will bring blessings to them for years. They are building for the future instead of trying to have it all right now. Seek the Lord and ask

Him what will be best for you. Like Abraham, we want to live under God's blessing and protection. Be careful what you wish for or you may lose it all.

- When have you looked back in life and wished that you had done things differently? What change would you make in the future?

19. Losing it all to the world
Gen. 19:23-35

Context: Lot had become part of Sodom and had adopted its culture. Both he and his wife find it hard to leave the comforts and wealth of the city. His daughters also show that they have become like Sodom by their solution for the future.

Where is your church? We tend to answer that by giving a physical address. My church is at the corner of First and Main. If you want to see it, you have to go there. The Bible doesn't define church as a place. It defines church as a people. The church is to be a people out in the world showing the character and the love of God. Yet, we have to be careful that we don't give up our character and become just part of the world. Pounded by the media and by our culture, too many Christians think and talk just like everyone else. If we are not careful, we will lose all the advantages of being a Christian by containing our faith within the walls of a church building. We lose the advantage of having God's character and values as we live out our lives.

Lot gave in to the culture of Sodom. He became one of

them and accepted their morals. Here was a place where visitors were expected to be given up to the crowds for forced rape. Violence was so common that Lot would not let the visitors stay out in the city square. Sadly, Lot had lost his morals and his character. We see that in his solution to protect the visitors. *"Look, I have two daughters who have never slept with a man. Let me bring them out to you and you can do what you like with them." (v.8)* Protecting the visitors was admirable, but to do so by sacrificing his daughters to the mob is not what any man of God would do. Trying to do something good, Lot proposed something evil. Lot had given into his world.

Mrs. Lot had given in to the city as well. Hesitant to leave the city, the "men" from God have to grasp her hand in order to get her and the others to leave the city. The message was simple. God is destroying this city. Flee for your lives. Don't look back and don't stop in the plain. You only have a short time. Yet, she had grown accustomed to this place with its allure and its riches. It was hard to leave behind all that she had worked so hard to have over the last couple of years. This was their home and there was no other place that she would rather be. In the end, *"Lot's wife looked back, and she became a pillar of salt." (v.26)* Slowing her pace because she struggled to leave the city, the destruction of the city caught up with her and destroyed her, too. Her heart was with the city and she could not bear to leave it.

The two daughters had been tainted by this wicked city. They settled in the mountains after the destruction of Sodom with their father. Having escaped the evil of the city, it was time to build a new life. One would have thought that Lot and the girls would have sought out suitable men to be husbands for the daughters. Touched by Sodom, the daughters come up with their own plan. *"Let's get our father to drink wine and then lie with him and preserve our family line through our father. (v.32)* With their moral compass damaged from years of living in Sodom, the daughters justify the unthinkable so that the family can go on. No one even thinks of going back to Abraham and marrying one of the servants. Godly options were available, but the daughters have an evil plan of their own.

One by one, the family had become like Sodom. God could

take Lot and his daughters out of Sodom, but Sodom was still in them. When Christians live just like the world, they can expect that they will have the same future as the world. Parents go to parties and get drunk and wonder why alcohol and drugs are prevalent among our children. We go to a football game on Sunday rather than a church service and wonder why our children see no reason to attend church or believe in God. When the world can't see any difference between the Christian and his non-Christian neighbor, we need to be worried. God's people are supposed to influence the culture not become the culture that they live in.

The blessings of being church are many. A family that worships the Lord and has devotions together is shaping the values of the whole family. This is a family that will care for each other. This is a family that will live by the morals of the Lord. The parents model what it means to belong to Jesus and the kids have the values ingrained in them. God becomes the priority for the whole family instead of football games and kids' soccer. This is a family that will live in the world but will have the attitudes and character of Christ. While it doesn't guarantee happiness, it helps the family not become part of

the culture or forget Christ.

- What is one thing that you are hesitant to give up from our

  society? How is that affecting you and your family?

20. Even saints sin
Genesis 20:1-5

Context: Shortly after the destruction of Sodom, Abraham moves south with his flocks. When Abraham moves south, He has some familiar fears and terrible solutions that will again cause him and others pain.

I am all too aware of my faults. I pray about them often in my prayers. I want so much to be rid of them, but I find that I struggle to overcome some of my sins. I bet you sin, too. Why are we amazed or even horrified when we hear about a Christian leader sinning? Why is the solution for the pastor or elder to step down from their ministry? Too many people expect that if the sinner leaves the church then all will be well. Sadly, this idea is so pervasive that ordinary people in the church feel like they cannot be forgiven either. The couple with marriage problems silently departs the church. The couple with the rowdy children slips out the back and hopes that their children will one day be perfect enough to allow them to come back to church. Truth is that we all sin. We all need help with our sin rather than being expected to be exempt from sin.

Abraham's sin all began when he moved into enemy territory. We read *"Now Abraham moved on from there into the region of the Negev and lived between Kadesh and Shur."* *(v.1)* After living safely in Hebron for about 20 years, Abraham moves to the area that will someday be the territory of the Philistines. Unlike the first time that he moved in Genesis 12, there is no reason given for this move. There was no famine or trouble with the neighbors. One wonders if Hebron was too close to the memories of Sodom. Perhaps Abraham found that the grazing land had become too thin. The text doesn't tell us why he left the place where he had come to know God. We just see him move from the safety of God's place for him into an area of danger that he was not ready for.

As soon as he went to Gerar, he began to be afraid. He began to walk by his wits and to tell lies. *"And there Abraham said of his wife Sarah, she is my sister." (v.2)* He was in a foreign land and he forgot the power of his God. He forgot that his God was not limited by area. He even forgot the promise that the Lord had made about Isaac only a few months before (Gen. 18:10). It was as if he moved and left his God behind.

Soon he was back to an old tactics of defense. He began to spread the lie that his wife was his sister. It was a lie that had caused him so much pain before. Now that lie would threaten the promise God had made about having a son.

This lie had caused Abraham's and Sarah's grief years before and the lie would cause them grief now. *"Then Abimelech, king of Gerar sent for Sarah and took her." (v.2)* Sarah is 89 and Abimelech wants her for his harem. A simple lie to save Abraham's skin has unanticipated consequences. We can only imagine what would have happened if the king had found her pregnant in his harem or if Isaac would not have been born at all because of this deception. Abraham put all of God's plans in jeopardy with a simple lie. He put his wife and his future in danger because he had not learned from the past. He finds himself in trouble and is probably unsure what to do next. He has forgotten to trust the Lord and will need God's help if he is to survive this ordeal.

What would have happened if God had abandoned Abraham at this point? Imagine the Bible story ending here with Sarah as another man's wife and Isaac never being born.

What would have happened to God's promise of the Messiah? The story will unfold as a story of grace. We will see how God works to reclaim the sinner Abraham and keep promises made to him. Our God is one who keeps His promises in spite of His people. He will expose the sin and let consequences come upon the sinner. He is also a God who is gracious and merciful to the sinner who repents. God's actions give us a pattern for dealing with our sins and the sins of others. The sin should be brought into the light, but it also should be forgiven when a person repents. God wants us to reclaim the sinner and not discard him.

Imagine a church gathering around a pastor who has committed adultery. As he tearfully confesses his sin to his wife and to the church, the congregation gathers around him in prayer. The church pays for marriage counseling to deal with the underlying problems. The church allows the pastor a few weeks off to focus on healing the marriage so that the church can welcome the man and his family back in ministry. The church will reclaim the man and his ministry. They will have a pastor and wife who will never forget what God's people have done for them. The years ahead can bring a

pastor who will serve with joy and will give the love back to his

people. Saints sin and saints can be forgiven by God.

- When have you felt like you were not good enough to be at

  church? How does this story let you know God still wants

  you?

21. The high cost of sinning
Genesis 20:6-13

Context: Abraham lies even though he has been told that the child of promise will come with within the next year (Chapter 18). Abimelech's desire for a "single" Sarah to be part of his harem puts God's promises in danger. God reacts quickly to save the promise He has made.

It's no big deal. How often have we heard someone speak of sin with those words? We want to excuse our sins and whisk them under the carpet. Yet, sin has consequences and sin hurts. You or I can say something untrue about a friend and it will haunt them for years. A night of drinking can cause a car crash leaving people paralyzed or dead. Our sin can destroy us and innocent people as well. Sin is powerful. Those who minimize sin or pretend that it does not exist will pay the consequences. It erodes our character and changes our future. God doesn't take sin lightly and neither should we. When we see what a simple sin can do, we will never think of it as "no big deal" again.

The Bible doesn't pull any punches. It always tells things

just like they are. Our "hero" Abraham looks pretty bad in this text. Isn't it odd that the pagan King Abimelech is the man of integrity in this story? He welcomes Abraham with open arms and is paid for his hospitality with a curse of barrenness. Even God admits *"Yes, I know you did this with a clear conscience and so I have kept you from sinning against me." (v.6)* Abraham has sinned and the pagan king and his household have paid the price. Ironically, the punishment was given with mercy in mind. God did these things so that the innocent Abimelech would not sin against God's plan without knowing it.

Sadly, our "hero" is not even gracious when he is caught in the act of sinning. He blames the very people who have been hurt by his sin. *"I said to myself, there is surely no fear of God in this place and they will kill me because of my wife." (v.11)* He then excuses his lie because it is half true. This is not Abraham's finest moment. God has shown Himself to the king as one who is powerful and merciful. Abraham has shown himself to be a self-centered liar. The good news is that hand of God is still working in the text. God does not give up on His servant or on the promises that He has made to Abraham. The dream given to King Abimelech is meant to salvage the promise of Isaac that would have been destroyed had the king been allowed to take Sarah into his harem forever.

While God did not defend the sin of his servant, He did bring honor back to Abraham. He made Abraham the mediator of restoration and grace. *"Now return the man's wife, for he is a prophet, and he will pray for you and you will live." (v.7)* The king will not give Abraham the punishment that he deserves for God has made it clear that Abraham's intercession is the thing that stands between the king and death. Abimelech brings sheep, cattle and slaves to Abraham in order to request his favor. God's healing in answer to Abraham's prayer (v.17) confirms the status of this fallen saint. God is still standing behind His servant. Ironically, the innocent pagan honors the fallen saint because of the true God.

Abraham's story reminds us that while God will always forgive those who repent, we often still face painful consequences to our sin. Gambling away our paycheck can be forgiven, but we still may lose the house and our family.

Lying to friends or family can be forgiven, but it will take a long time before they trust us again. The effects of sin can last for years even with repentance. God will wipe away the sin with the power of the cross, but it may take us a long time, even with God's help, to put life back together. We should never doubt the power of sin and its lasting effects in our lives or in the lives of others.

While we will never be without sin, we can learn from past mistakes. A near accident while drunk should teach us to stay sober. A large loss in gambling should make us stay away from the casino. Abraham and Sarah had lied to Egypt's pharaoh years before (Gen 13) with disastrous results. Now they face the same pain again. The wise will respect the danger of sin. They will learn from past mistakes and the mistakes of others. As we learn from our sins, we will find that the pain of repeating sins can be avoided with the power of the Lord. God will help us build our lives and families as we repent of sin and seek His help to avoid them in the future. The high cost of sin doesn't have to overwhelm us if we will learn from past mistakes with God's help.

- What sin does the most damage in your life? What is one thing you could do with God's help to limit its effect?

22. The fruit of patience
Genesis 21: 1-17

Context: Isaac's birth brings joy and conflict. Twenty-five years (Gen. 12:4) after Abraham left Haran for the Promised Land, the child of promise is born. His name reflects the laughter and joy that he brings to Sarah.

Patience isn't easy. We live in a "microwave" generation that wants everything now. Often, we want God to work the same way. I have watched Christians waiting by the side of a parent's bedside praying for immediate healing. I have watched couples wonder when the Lord will bless them with their first child. In those times, we wonder why we have to wait. We have to learn to trust the Lord and believe that there is a reason for the waiting. It may that we need to grow. It may be that God has other pieces to put in place or that God wants something to happen at a certain time for maximum effect. It isn't easy waiting, but those who learn to be patient and wait on the Lord will find that the result is worth the wait. God always has a reason for His timing.

"Abraham was a hundred years old when his son Isaac

was born to him." (v.5) Twenty-five years have passed since the call of Abraham in Genesis 12. During that time, Abraham has prospered under the hand of God. The man called from Ur has vast flocks and a mighty army of his own men. Yes, there were mishaps along the way, but mostly there was faith. Abraham and Sarah have kept their faith in the spectacular promises of an unseen God. From time to time, God would speak to encourage the couple. In between those times, the promises must have seemed like a long time coming. Now the promise was fulfilled. They could hold the son, the father of children as numerous as the sky, in their hands. Faith had been rewarded. They had trusted the Almighty God to keep these amazing promises and God had come through.

That an elderly man and woman could have a baby was a miracle. The answer to how this was possible was simple. *"Now the Lord was gracious to Sarah as he had said." (v.1)* God seemed to have a purpose in waiting to fulfill His promise. A child earlier in life would have seemed normal. This child would show God's power to the world and to future generations. Isaac became a reminder that God could and would do the impossible. The time also gave Abraham and Sarah a chance to grow in their faith. Now, they were spiritual people who trusted in the Lord instead of seeking their own solutions. Isaac's birth demonstrated God's commitment and love to them. It taught them that that all the other promises which seemed impossible could and would come true.

Their patience was rewarded with joy. *"Sarah said, God has brought me laughter and everyone who hears about this will laugh with me." (v.6)* Joy and laughter had come to this house. The child was the first step in God's fulfillment of all the promises. Here was the child whose descendants would own the land of Palestine. Here was the child that the Lord would use to make Abraham's name be great and bless the whole world. None of those promises felt real before the birth of the child. Now the future had come. God's plan was concrete. It had form and flesh. It was real, and it encouraged them to believe all the other promises would be kept after they had both passed away. Their patient faith had seen that God would and did keep His promises.

We mentally know that God always keeps His promises,

yet it is hard to be patient and wait for the promises to be fulfilled. We can easily forget what God has promised or let our heart be swayed into doubting that the promise will really come. We can cause ourselves great discomfort and troubles as we try to fix things like Abraham did with Ishmael. When worry replaces faith, we can cause pain for ourselves and others. Those who will continue to wait for the Lord will see that the Lord does fulfill His promises every time. He often fulfills promises in ways greater than we ever expected. Be patient and give God the time to do a miracle that will bring joy to you and to others.

I will warn you that patience will change you. A patient man knows to pray through a crisis instead of making himself sick with worry. A patient woman will reach out to help others as she confidently waits for the Lord instead of expecting the world to stop and care for her. Patience is a fruit of faith. As faith grows, we trust God more in life and will find that trust rewarded. Patient faith sees God's hand in the crisis and trusts Him. Patient faith believes that God will help us because He loves us and wants to help us in every situation. As patience grows, we can learn to let the Lord direct us through all the tough situations in life.

- What "impossible thing" could God do for you now? What can God do in your situation that you cannot do?

23. Difficult Choices
Genesis 21: 8-21

Context: Abraham now has two sons and two mothers who cannot get along. Abraham must make a choice in line with God's promises. Ishmael, whom Abraham loves, must be sent packing so that Isaac may thrive, and the covenant can be fulfilled.

Life is filled with choices. Some choices are simple and have little consequence. "Do I want the beef or the chicken tonight?" Other choices will change your whole life. "Do I go to college or to trade school?" "Is this the right person to get married to or do I wait for another?" Choices that change the course of your whole life can be extremely hard to make. How do you know what to do when you face difficult or painful choices? How do you make a choice when your heart is torn in both directions? God has the answers if we will ask Him our questions. Sometimes, the choice is clearer when something is right or wrong. Sometimes the choice is easier if we weigh the pros and cons. I have found that we often just need to pray and ask the Lord for His direction when the choices get tough. That is exactly what Abraham did.

Sadly, Isaac and Ishmael can't live together. Isaac is two or three years old at the time of weaning. Ishmael is now about 16 or 17. An infant who may or may not live is not a threat to big brother Ishmael. Yet, a baby brother who is thriving and who will inherit everything threatens an older brother who thought he would be the heir. A strong young man like Ishmael begins to lash out at the child and mock him. He asserts his claim as the first born of Abraham's family to anyone who will listen. Sarah notices and starts to complain to Abraham. *"But Sarah saw that the son whom Hagar the Egyptian had borne to Abraham was mocking." (v.9)* Ishmael wants his place in the family as the first-born son. Sarah wants to make sure that her son is the heir.

"The matter distressed Abraham greatly because it concerned his son." (v.11) It broke Abraham's heart. He loved Ishmael. Ishmael was, after all, his son. Abraham has had years to watch Ishmael grow. He wants his children to get along and be one big happy family. Yet, Ishmael has caused a

rift that cannot be healed. God knows that Ishmael will be a "wild donkey of a man" who will "live in hostility toward all his brothers" (Gen. 16:12). Sarah's concerns are real, but that doesn't make it easy for Abraham. The two sons cannot coexist together, and Abraham has to make a choice. Sarah wants Ishmael to go. How can a man turn his back on his son?

I picture Abraham lifting up his voice to God in prayer. Abraham has learned to come to the Lord for help. God's answer is clear, but that still doesn't make the solution easy. *'Listen to whatever Sarah tells you because it is through Isaac that your offspring will be reckoned." (v.12)* Isaac is the child of promise and the one who would receive all of God's blessings. Ishmael is the son of the maidservant and must go as Sarah says. God will lessen the pain. He will make Ishmael into a great nation because of God's love for Abraham. As hard as it must have been, Abraham listened to his God. He gave Hagar and Ishmael a few supplies and then sent them off into the desert. The son of the covenant stays. The son of the flesh must go. The two cannot exist together and Abraham knows it.

He must trust the Lord who has promised to care for the boy.

Making choices is painful. Sometimes there are patterns in our life needing to be shown the door. It might be a bad habit like smoking or overeating. It might be a sin like gossip or lust. Sometimes it is simply a change in course. We want to take a new job, but it means leaving a home and city we have come to love. Where can we turn for help? Where can we find answers when we face difficult questions? We can turn to the Lord for His wisdom and strength. He can help us see what is best for us when our emotions are torn. He can give us strength to take a choice that may not be easy for us. The Lord will help those who pray to Him so that they have the strength and courage to make the difficult choices.

The joy of seeking out the Lord brings peace to our decisions. If we believe that the Lord is always right and follow Him, we can confidently move forward. We do not have to second guess ourselves. We know that our God will lead us to make right choices. Such choices still may be hard like Abraham's choice. Yet, we walk away knowing that we have done the right thing. We don't have to second guess the choice for years. We make the choice and live confident that the Lord will help us to succeed at the choice we have made.

- If you had one area of your life that you would choose to change, what would it be? How would making the change affect your life?

24. God Never Forgets a Promise
Genesis 21: 14-21

Context: Ishmael's departure seems harsh, but God has not

forgotten the promises that he made to Hagar in chapter 16.

Ishmael will survive and be the father of a great nation

because of God's love for Abraham.

We all forget things. People forget where they put their car

keys or forget their wife's birthday. People give up on a pledge

that they have made to lose weight and forget things that they

promised to do for someone else. Sadly, we cause ourselves

the greatest grief when we forget God and His blessings. We

find ourselves in crisis and forget to pray. We find ourselves

wondering what to do and don't think to look for answers in

His word. We complain that we are all alone, but God is eager

to help and has made dozens of promises to that effect.

Fortunately, when we forget God, He doesn't forget us.

Sometimes, He even breaks into our lives so that we

remember the love and promises that He will never forget.

Sad and disheartened, Hagar is ready to give up. *"She*

went off and sat down nearby, about a bowshot away; for she thought I cannot watch the boy die." (v.16) Having been kicked

out of Abraham's house, Hagar gets lost in the wilderness. In

the desert, she soon runs out of food and water. She feels that

life is over and that she and the boy will surely die.

Unfortunately, she has forgotten the promises that the Lord

made to her in Genesis 16. Even before the child was born,

God had promised that Ishmael would have descendants too

numerous to count. Years had elapsed since that day, but

God had not forgotten His promise. His promise to her was

still good. Hagar could have saved herself a lot of pain if she

had just remembered what God had promised.

Fortunately, God has not forgotten her. *"What is the matter*

Hagar? Do not be afraid; God has heard the boy crying as he

lies there." (v.17) The Lord had heard the cry of Ishmael.

Whether it is a cry of pain or the prayer of a heart searching

for God, we don't know. God would rescue them for

Abraham's sake. God would keep His promise. He opens

Hagar's eyes so that she sees the life-giving water nearby.

She immediately fills her water skin and gives her son a drink.

God will not let them die but will care for them just as He had promised. Hagar had forgotten God, but God would not forget her. Hagar needed faith in the promises of God. She needed to get ready for the future that God had promised to her years before. God will not allow her and her son to die in this place.

God then reaffirms His promise for the future. *"Lift the boy up and take him by the hand, for I will make him into a great nation."(v.18)* It is the promise that God had made years before. It is the promise that God had reaffirmed to Abraham just a short time ago (v.13). Hagar is to lift up her son in faith and to trust the Lord just as Abraham had. Ishmael will have a bright future. God will be with the boy as he grows up. They can depend on the Lord to care for them and to make a great nation of this child of Abraham. They are to trust the Lord as He helps them build a new future. God will be with them in the years to come. Ishmael will grow to be a strong man who will have many descendants just as God promised.

It was not easy for Hagar to start again when she left the home of Abraham. Hagar made the situation worse because she forgot the promise of God. Many people make life harder because they forget God in times of need. We think that problems mean that God has forgotten us or that God doesn't like us. We forget the simple truth. We live in a sinful world where we will all face problems. God is the one person that we can depend on when times are bad. The scripture is filled with promises from God. As we remember them, we can cry out to God for His help in prayer just as Hagar should have. There is no reason to forget the Lord and just put up with things till we die. Call upon Him in the midst of trouble. God never forgets a promise.

Life changes when we listen to God's promises in scripture and believe them. Instead of wandering through our "desert", we seek direction from God. Instead of trying to solve problems with our limited resources, we call on the one who created the world and has infinite resources to rebuild lives torn apart by lost jobs, illness or family problems. Our Lord can turn our despair into joy. Those who seek out God's promises and live by them will find that life is filled with hope. We may forget God, but God never forgets the promises that He makes. His promises are good forever and we would be wise to claim them every day of our lives.

- Name one promise that God makes in the Bible to His people. Ask God to bring that promise to completion in your life.

25. God's Man
Genesis 21: 22-34

Context: Abraham had lied to Abimelech (Chapter 20), but now it is Abraham's time to stand tall and strong as the two of them negotiate a treaty. Abraham claims a well and plants a tree as signs that he believes God's promise that his descendants will inherit this land.

"Sorry, I didn't mean to tell a dirty joke, pastor. I forgot that you were here." There are times that I get tired of having people act differently when I am near and hold me to higher standards. Yet every Christian should have those problems in life. The world around us should see a difference in your life if you are a Christian. Christians should be more honest, more loving, and less likely to cheat or steal. People shouldn't be comfortable lying or swearing in front of a Christian. Trouble is that a lot of Christians don't live that way and the world has noticed. Non-Christians often don't want to belong to a church that seems no different than the world because they see no advantage in it. They think that faith in God has very little impact on our lives and offers very little help. It begs the question, "What should it look like when Christians belong to God?"

Abraham was becoming a wealthy and powerful man. King Abimelech comes to Abraham wanting assurance that Abraham will deal honestly with him and not lie as he had done before. He seems concerned because he has begun to notice something powerful about Abraham's life. *"God is with you in everything you do." (v.22)* The power of God was evident in God's protection of Abraham and Sarah during that sin. The power of God has also been evident in the years since. Abraham has prospered greatly among the king's people. Abraham also has been given the miracle of a son late in life. God's hand has been evident as He did miraculous things. Abimelech has noticed all these things and wants a pledge of honesty and friendship from one who lives in his territory and who has such a powerful God.

Abimelech's words show that Abraham has become God's man to the people around him. He will demonstrate God's character by the way that he handles controversy. Water in the wilderness area of Palestine means life or death. You could not just stand back and let someone take such a vital resource. With hundreds of servants, Abraham could have taken matters into his own hands when his well was taken. Abraham, the man of God, treats Abimelech with honor and decides to go to him to settle the problem. His method, *"Then Abraham complained to Abimelech about a well of water that Abimelech's servants had seized" (v.25)* shows that he respects the king. His patience shows him to be a man of God who has learned to deal wisely with others and to trust the Lord.

Abraham also shows himself to be a man of God by publicly acknowledging the Lord before the world. We see that *"Abraham planted a tamarisk tree in Beersheba and there he called upon the name of the Lord." (v.33)* Abraham does not hide his faith but plants a tree as a memorial to his God. Abraham's God was an everlasting God and the tree, while not everlasting, will proclaim to generations the nature and love of his God. The tree would also serve to remind Abraham that the peace and prosperity that he now enjoys are a gift from the Almighty God whom he serves. He belongs to God and will live as God's man. He will deal with others in the strength and the honesty of the Lord.

Being God's man or woman is often seen as a burden with lots of rules to keep and lots of people to help. As we see in the life of Abraham, it is not a burden but a great blessing. Abraham was respected by the king because he was a man of God. To this pagan king, Abraham represented the power and character of God. His faith allowed the Lord to work with such authority and miracles that the pagan king could not doubt that they had come from an Almighty God. Abraham's character allowed him to be a blessing to others and to live in peace with them because they could trust him. You couldn't miss God's imprint on Abraham.

The men and women of God will find that life improves when they live in the power and character of God. Those who trust in the Lord and depend on the Lord to help them will find that the Lord can do far more than they can do by themselves. Those who live with the Lord's character will gain the respect of others as God makes them a blessing to the people around them. God's men and women have an advantage in this world.

God works in their lives and gives them a code of values that helps them know right from wrong. The values steer them clear of the dangers that often destroy others. The change is so great that others notice the hand of the Lord in our lives and the blessings that God alone can bring.

- How would you define "God's man or woman"? Can the people around you at your work or neighborhood tell you belong to God? What sets you apart?

26. Entrusting Your Children to God
Gen. 22:1-19

Context: Isaac is a teenager and Abraham is well over 110 years old. God calls Abraham to do the unthinkable. The faith of Abraham and his trust in God is shown in his willingness to put the life of his son in God's hands.

As a pastor, I have always felt the strain of family versus ministry. There was the birthday party that I missed because of a funeral and there was the funeral I missed because of the birth of one of my children. Most people I know face the problem of balancing work with family as well. There are weeks where we just can't help working 60 or more hours. There are also weeks where one of the kids gets sick and your job has to take second place. How does service for the Lord fit in to all of that? How do we manage the times when God calls us to put Him first? It maybe that He asks you to take on a project at church or help a neighbor. Are we willing to sacrifice the things that are most important to us? Are we willing to give our precious time to God so that He can make life for us and others better?

Abraham had waited for 25 years for this son. He knew that all the promises of God depended on Isaac. If Isaac was gone, there would be no descendants as numerous as the stars and no one to inherit the land. Surely, Isaac's life was more precious to Abraham than his own life. God came to him with a command that no one wants to hear. *"Take your son, your only son, Isaac, . sacrifice him there as a burnt offering"* *(v.2)* It was a test to see how much Abraham loved his God. Abraham was being asked to sacrifice the greatest thing that God had given him because he trusted the Lord. The birth of his son was a miracle from the Lord and now Abraham was being asked to put that miracle back into God's hands.

God didn't ask Abraham to take his son and sacrifice him immediately. It would have been easier to strike Isaac down quickly while you had your nerve. Abraham was called to make a long journey to the sacred mountain. It was *"on the third day Abraham looked up and saw the place in the distance." (v.4)* The three-day journey gave Abraham plenty of time to turn back and refuse what must have seemed to be a cruel request. Here, there would be no wife or servants to stop him from completing the task. Here he would have to fight only his own desires as he sacrificed his son. Abraham had to make a choice to go, to climb the mountain and finally to strike his son. No one could stop or encourage him in the task. This was a test of his faith and his love for God.

In the end, he was willing to give back to the Lord the greatest gift that he had received. *"Then he reached out his hand and took the knife to slay his son." (v.10)* He believed in the promises of God so much that he trusted that God would give his son back to him somehow. What God would do with the sacrifice, Abraham did not know. He could only trust God and know that his God had always loved him and would keep the promises He had made about this son. How it affected Isaac to see that his father loved God more than his own son is hard to guess. Yet, that act spoke volumes to the young patriarch about what real worship was and how important God was to their future.

Abraham was willing to give up his most precious gift, his son, to the Lord. In that moment, God changed Abraham and Isaac. Abraham saw the love of the Lord and how important both he and his future were to the Lord. Isaac saw the depth of his father's love for the Lord and had a sense of what faith in God meant. As we give our lives and the lives of our children to the Lord; they will be forever changed as well. God will bless our lives as we dedicate them to Him so that they will be productive in ways that we cannot imagine. God will bless our children as we bring them to Him in faith. They will learn to respect and love the Lord as we have. He will build a lasting relationship with them and will give them character and purpose for their lives.

I imagine that the teenage Isaac walked down the mountain a different person. He had heard the voice of God, seen God's provision and seen the depth of his father's love for God. When we entrust our children to God, it changes them. They have a character and values that give them an edge in life. As parents show the depth of their faith in weekly worship and daily devotions, children set patterns that they can keep for life. When God comes before Sunday morning sports or evening television; your children will notice. The Lord becomes a greater part of their lives so that God has a greater opportunity to protect and guide them in life. Giving our greatest gift to God does not mean that we lose them. Such action entrusts our children to the care and protection of the only one who can truly help them succeed.

- What would you like your children to learn about God? How would a closer relationship with the Lord impact their life and their future?

27. Teaching By Trial
Gen. 22:1-19

Context: It was a three-day journey from Beersheba to Mt. Moriah giving Abraham a lot of time to think and to refuse God's command. He will learn about God's love for him and grow in his faith through this test.

A lot of Christians think that life is supposed to be smooth and easy just because we are Christians. If there are troubles, it means that something must be wrong. We begin to complain to God that He has let us down. That is especially true if trouble comes in our service for the Lord. "I witnessed to my neighbor like you told me to, why did it go so badly?" "I am just trying to be a good parent; do you think you could help Lord?" Troubles are seen as an inconvenience that should never happen to a Christian. Troubles make us wonder about God's love. Rather, we need to see that God allows trials in order to teach us. Lot never had trials, but Abraham had several in his lifetime. Lot was so stuck in the world and its sin that God never had a chance to teach him like God taught Abraham. God's hand can be seen in Abraham's trials and in the blessings that come from them.

Trials can be used to teach us to obey and follow God's commands. *"Early the next morning Abraham got up and saddled his donkey" (v.3)* If God is to teach us, we must be in the right place. Abraham could have refused to take the journey and the lesson would never have happened. Instead, he makes a painful three-day journey to Moriah as the Lord commands. It was at Moriah where the lesson was to take place. We often think that we have a right to demand God solve our problems and help us with our needs on our schedule and where we think that we want it to happen. The truth is that only when we have obeyed the Lord and are in the place that He has called us to be will we see the Lord meet our needs.

God not only chooses the place, but the time. Isaac is tied up and laying on the altar with the knife in Abraham's hand ready to strike. Only at the last minute does the Lord provide for His servant. *"But the angel of the Lord called out to him from heaven." (v.11)* The lesson has had its full effect. God could have tested Abraham after one day of the journey or even at the foot of the mountain. Yet, it was only when the lesson was complete that the Lord provided an answer. He wanted Abraham to both know and act as if he believed that the Lord would provide the lamb for the burnt offering. We don't get to quit in the middle of a math exam and God will not allow us to quit in the middle of His trials.

When the time and place are right, God often provides an ordinary answer. *"Abraham looked up and there in a thicket he saw a ram caught by its horns." (v.13)* God could have sent an angel down from heaven with a lamb or miraculously made one appear before Abraham. Yet, God often does things in a way that are natural. In this case, He simply allowed a ram to get caught in a bush by its horns. Some would call it coincidence, it was so unobtrusive. Yet we know that it was God's way of providing. Abraham needed an animal for the altar that he had built, and God arranged for him to have one at the very moment that he needed it. We often look for God to provide in spectacular ways, but our God often uses the ordinary things of life given at just the right moment.

It is in the trials of life that faith becomes real and stronger.

Throughout his journey, Abraham had voiced that "God would provide the lamb". Yet, it is through the trial that Abraham learned that his trust was not ill founded. We know in our mind that God wants our neighbor to hear the gospel and that God wants His church to serve the community, but it is often only when we step out and do that ministry that we find out how much we can depend on God. Faith does not demand explanations. It rests on the promises of God and believes in His provision.

Life changes when we act on the promises of God instead of demanding explanations. Churches move forward into their community to help and serve even when they don't have all the resources in place. Christians witness to their friends and neighbors even when they are not sure what to say. We know God wants this ministry done and are sure He will provide what is needed at the proper time. Life will not be easy. God knows that we need His trials to get us ready for the things that we cannot control. As we grow in faith, God will overcome the troubles and crisis that bring others to their knees. As we grow in faith, God will use us to help others and make a huge impact on our world. Explanations are not given before we begin because we often would not believe them. Provision is given at the right time so that we trust God to do the impossible.

- What impossible thing is God calling you to do right now? What holds you back? What will you ask God to provide?

28. A Good Marriage
Gen. 23:1-19

Context: The cave of Machpelah still exists in the city of

Hebron today. It stands below a mosque built over the site. In

the tomb you can see the burial places of Abraham, Sarah,

Isaac, Rebekah, Jacob and Leah.

I can't imagine life without my wife Joan. We have been

married for over 35 years and have three grown children. Life

would not be the same without her. I am sure that many of you

feel the same about your spouse. Over the years, I have

watched the tears shed at a funeral as someone buries their

spouse. Maybe they give a final kiss or touch of the face

before they close the casket on the one, they love. It is

obvious that there will be a hole in their lives that will never

quite heal. We often feel sorrow for the spouse left behind, but

we should also feel joy for the years that they had together. A

strong marriage is a gift from the Lord. God intended that we

have this lifelong relationship. It is God's hope that our vows at

God's altar develop into a relationship lasting 50 or 60 years. It

is one of the greatest gifts that the Lord can give us.

You can feel the tears on Abraham's face. *"Abraham went to mourn for Sarah and to weep over her." (v.2)* Abraham has lost his soul mate. After 127 years, she is gone. Abraham will live for 38 more years after her death (Genesis 25:7), but it will not be the same. We often tell people not to cry at a funeral, but the tears of Abraham honor his wife and show how important she was to him. She is the wife that came with him to the Palestine to claim God's promise. She is the mother of Isaac who was a miracle from God. Abraham will remarry and have additional children in his old age, but it is Sarah who he will lie by in death. A great blessing is now gone in his life.

Abraham takes pains to bury her in Palestine and not back in Ur of the Chaldeans. *"Sell me some property for a burial site here so I can bury my dead." (v.4)* This is their home and their place that God has given them. Her burial in Hebron signaled Abraham's faith in the promise that the Lord had given this land to their descendants. She should be buried here where her family would live for centuries. She should be buried here so that others of her family could join her when they die. Over the years, that came to be reality. The cave where Sarah was buried in Hebron would also contain the bodies of Abraham, Isaac, Rebecca, Jacob and Leah. While Abraham would have to buy a place to bury Sarah, he believed that this would be their home. Sarah's tomb would become beach head for the future. The tomb was an act of faith claiming God's promise for himself and his family.

Nothing is too good for Sarah. Abraham has his eye on the cave of Machpelah and the field that goes with it. Nothing else will do. *"Intercede with Ephron son of Zohar on my behalf so he will sell me the cave of Machpelah which belongs to him."* *(v.8-9)* Arriving at a final price for a piece of property usually involved a great deal of bargaining. Yet, Abraham calmly announces what he wants and that he will pay full price for the land. One would expect shrewdness, but Sarah had been so precious to Abraham that he wanted the best for her. He agrees to buy both the cave and the field even before Ephron names the price. His concern is not to get a good deal, but to honor his wife. He seals the deal by paying the 400 shekels of silver in the presence of the witnesses. The cave would belong to Sarah no matter what the price.

Marriages often are taken for granted only to be empty in our later years of life. We focus on raising our children or working at our careers. When the children move out, two strangers find that they barely know each other. We struggle to recapture the magic that we once had. We feel empty and feel like life just isn't what it used to be. Such is the power of marriage. A strong marriage is a joy for a couple every day. It provides a friend who we enjoy traveling with, having hobbies with or just sitting and watching the sunsets together. A weak marriage is a daily grind where two people push and shove for dominance and often avoid each other. The picture of Abraham and Sarah is God's hope for all of us. He wants us to have that joy.

No matter how strong or weak your marriage, think of what it would have been like to have Abraham and Sarah's marriage. Think of being so close to your spouse that you shed the tears of Abraham at his or her funeral. The joy that such a marriage gives is priceless. It is God's gift of a friend, a partner, and a helper in life. It is never too late. Court your spouse again. Carve out time for just the two of you whether you have children at home or not so that you can know each other and talk at a deeper level. As you support and spend time with them, you can change the quality of your life and of your legacy.

- What can you learn from Abraham about love in marriage? What is one thing you can do to show your love for your spouse today?

29. Tough Assignment
Genesis 24:1-14

Context: The servant gets the tough assignment to make a journey of hundreds of miles over several months leading a caravan of ten camels. This is a story of Abraham's trust in God and a servant who depends on the Lord as well.

As a parent, I wanted my children to excel. I supported them in high school and in college. I encouraged them to do their best. Some of their success in life is because of the support that my wife and I gave them. It allowed them to push harder and to take risks. In this, we were not special. We did what any parent would do for their children. It is what a heavenly Father wants for His children as well. Yet, too many Christians hold back in ministry and play it safe. They plan and do ministry using their own resources and skills and never include God in the ministry that He gave them. God purposely gives tough assignments to His children so that they learn to trust Him to accomplish what they cannot do. He gives tough assignments so that we need His hand to complete the ministry that He has given us.

Abraham asked an impossible task of his trusted servant. Go to a strange land and bring back a wife for Isaac. While the task may seem difficult, it was a request based on the promise of God. *"He (God) will send His angel before you so that you can get a wife for my son from there." (v.7)* Abraham believes the promises of the Lord. He knows that the angel of the Lord will help the servant complete this task. God will be with him and God is ready to make the impossible happen. Abraham knows that God wants this mission to be completed successfully. Isaac is central to the plans and promises of the Lord. He needs the right wife so that God's future can proceed. Abraham sends the servant trusting the Lord will give success. He encourages the servant to trust the Lord as well.

Since this is God's task, the servant begins with prayer. *"Then he prayed, O Lord, God of my master Abraham, give me success today and show kindness to my master Abraham." (v.12).* This is a man of faith and he understands that there will be no success without the Lord's help. He could have asked people where he could find Abraham's family. He could have interviewed women of the family to find a suitable wife for Isaac. He does none of those things. Instead, he begins with prayer. He asks the Lord for success claiming the promise that God had made to Abraham. Only the eyes of God could spot which woman was the best for Isaac. He lays the mission in God's hands. The success of the venture depends on the Lord.

In his prayer, he asks for a sign. *"May it be that when I say to a girl, please let down your jar that I may have a drink. . . let her be the one you have chosen for your servant Isaac." (v.14)* In humility, he asks for a sign so that the Lord may choose the right woman. The bride of Isaac is to be the Lord's choice. He is only the tool that God will use. He believes so strongly in the promise that the Lord has made that he expects the Lord will direct him to the right woman. He will not act rashly or try to find her. He will wait patiently for the Lord to reveal His choice by the use of this sign. Somewhere among the thousands of women in this place is God's choice. God will bring her to the servant because God has promised success.

God gives tough assignments to His people, but He also gives His help. As we face those tough assignments, the servant shows us the way of success. Seek out and believe in God's promises. Look in the pages of scripture to see what God wants done in this situation. We want to let God reveal His direction and choice for our ministry. Pray for God's help so that you may be able to complete the task with His power and not your own meager resources. Finally, wait with confidence for the Lord. Ask for a sign if you feel that you need direction but let the Lord lead and reveal His choice. If the ministry is truly the Lord's ministry, He will bring success because He wants to impact others around you with His love and His gospel message.

Imagine what it would be like to be in a church where God's people believe, pray and wait for Him. Such a congregation would be powerful and would touch a lot of lives for the Lord because they are doing ministry based on God's direction and God's power. Prayer would bathe the ministry and give direction and the muscle to do even the toughest assignments. People would not be hasty or worry about whether the ministry is working. They would patiently wait together for the direction and guidance of the Lord. Our Father in heaven wants to do the unexpected in ministry among us.

He wants us to do things that people think are impossible. He

will do that as we draw close to Him in faith and depend on

Him to work miracles through us. Tough assignments are not

tough for Him. When God's people trust Him and are led by

Him, there is literally nothing that they cannot do.

- What need is present in your church or community that just

  seems impossible? Pray for God's answer and visualize

  how your ministry could change lives.

30. Knowing When to Say Yes
Gen. 24:15-67

Context: Time is short, and the journey home is long. The servant's hurry puts pressure on the family. Rebekah is faced with a choice that will change her life and her future.

The dream job offer is on the table before you. Do you say yes or is it too good to be true? He asks you to marry him. You really like him, but is he "the one"? Opportunities can come and go in an instant. How do we know whether to say yes or whether to pass them by? We can rely on our own senses and make judgments from them. A better way is to seek out the Lord and ask the Lord for help when we are considering a change. We might also ask ourselves if this is something that would be pleasing to the Lord. Life is full of God given opportunities because our God loves His people. Such opportunities can be fearful, but if we seek the Lord, we can gain the confidence to move in new directions with Him.

Abraham's servant had asked for a sign from God. Even before his prayer is complete, a beautiful woman appeared. He had asked for a sign from the Lord and the woman showed kindness and compassion in exactly the way that the servant had asked the Lord in his request. *"After she had given him a drink, she said, I'll draw water for your camels too." (v.19)* As he watched the young woman water the camels, he may have wondered if his mission was already successful. He became sure of it when he found out that the young lady was the granddaughter of Abraham's brother. God had answered his prayer and led him to this opportunity. He had no doubt what He needed to do. As he talks to the family, he gives credit to the Lord and tells the family how the Lord had led him to Rebekah.

The hand of the Lord was obvious to the family, but they were also cautious. They made a simple request. *"Let the girl remain with us ten days or so, then you may go." (v.55)* It was natural that they would want to spend time with her before she left them and lived hundreds of miles away. This was a great opportunity, but you sense that they wanted to be cautious before agreeing to the proposal. Could they trust this stranger? Did he really represent their Uncle Abraham? They considered the opportunity for their daughter to be the bride of a wealthy man. It was a chance for great wealth and the prospect of marriage to someone of their clan. As they listened to the story, they wanted to say yes, but they wavered as they struggled to trust God's direction.

They ultimately gave the final decision to Rebekah. She had heard the words about Abraham and Isaac. She had seen the proof of his greatness and wealth. What did she think? *"So they called Rebekah and asked her, will you go with this man? I will go, she said." (v.58)* She knew that she could weigh the pros and cons for several days, but ultimately her answer was just to trust God. The events showed that God had chosen Rebekah to be the wife of Isaac. It was up to Rebekah to make this choice for herself. She had to trust the Lord and be willing to put her life and her future in God's hands. It was all about saying yes to God's opportunity. The minute she said yes, she became part of God's plan of salvation for the whole world. The opportunity was great, and we remember her today because of her choice.

Opportunities are filled with great blessings and potential dangers. Opportunities also do not last forever. At times we can prepare for opportunities like the servant does. We have a need and we pray to the Lord for signs, so we know what the opportunity looks like when it comes. Other times, we have to prepare ourselves by being in the word and in prayer so that when God's opportunities come, we can hear the small still voice of God in the possibility. In either case, we weigh the opportunity in the balance of God's values. We can immediately say no if the opportunity would cause us to sin or to go against our values and personality. God will never call us to do something wrong or something He has not created us to do.

Rebekah saw the opportunity and acted on faith. She chose to believe, like her family, that *"This is from the Lord."* *(v.50)* She would have missed the greatest opportunity of her life if she had given in to fear and said no. As we walk through life, God will present opportunities for us as well. We can weigh them with human knowledge or we can judge opportunities by what we learn in the Bible and in prayer. Only with the lens of God's wisdom and by hearing God's small still voice can we have the insight to pass on opportunities that will hurt us and the courage to accept God's blessings that will change our lives.

- What opportunities are being presented in your life right now? What sign could you ask from God to help you follow His way?

31. Full of Years
Gen. 25:1-9

Context: Abraham's life did not end when Sarah died, or Isaac was married. He remarries and has six more children as he lives to the ripe old age of 175. He is a model for all of us who think that are productive years are behind us.

Old age doesn't have to mean empty years. The Lord continues to walk beside us and to bless us even as we age. He has tasks for us to do and life for us to live. Many people retire at age 65 with no plan for the future other than a desire not to work. A better plan might be to slow down but use retirement to take on a new career or volunteer ministry. Older adults are in a rare position to let retirement income pay the bills while they work at something that will be fulfilling and will benefit people. God does not desert us. God continues to be with His servants throughout their entire lives. He continues to bless us and give us opportunities to serve Him and others no matter what our age. Abraham shows himself to be one who is busy to the end.

Many think that the story of Abraham ends with Isaac

taking a wife. The torch has passed to the next generation. I am not sure that Abraham thinks that way. *"Abraham took another wife, whose name was Keturah. She bore him Zimran, Jokshan, Medan, Midian, Ishbak and Shuah." (v.1-2)* Abraham was 137 years old when Sarah died (Gen. 23:1), but that did not stop him from continuing in life. He remarried and had six more children including Midian, the father of the Midianites of Moses' time. God continued to bless Abraham all his life. Just because Sarah had died, or Isaac was now on his own did not mean that life was over. Abraham would live 38 more seemingly productive years.

The blessing of the Lord brought both quantity and quality to his life. *"Then Abraham breathed his last and died at a good old age, an old man and full of years and he was gathered to his people." (v.8)* He is described as dying "full of years". There was quality to his life. This was not a wilted man living on the charity of others. This was a man who proudly looked back on what the Lord had done. He could remember his walk with the Lord and the joys that the Lord had brought. He was a man who could look around and see what the Lord had done for him with large herds and a large family. He was also a man who could look ahead knowing God's promises were going to be fulfilled and that the Lord would be with him even in death. His life was full. God was an active part of his life from beginning to the end.

When life was ending, Abraham made sure that the torch did pass to Isaac. *"Abraham left everything he owned to Isaac. But while he was still living, he gave gifts to the sons of his concubines." (v.5-6)* Perhaps the Lord had given Abraham a clue that the end was near. Maybe it just seemed time as he came close to being 175 years old. He had followed the Lord for the last 100 years. He wanted to make sure that the legacy the Lord had given him would not be in danger. He gave everything to Isaac. God had named him the son of the promise. The six sons of Keturah were given gifts and ultimately sent away to the east. No one was to challenge Isaac. Nothing was to get in the way of God's covenant line.

When you come near the end of your life, how will you judge whether life was good or not? Most people agree that having lots of money in the bank or even the freedom to do anything you want does not mean much. Abraham gives us the real measure of success. Abraham could joyfully look back at his walk with the Lord and feel blessed at all that God has done for him. He then could look forward and build on that foundation by serving the Lord and others till the end of life. The full life of Abraham came because God was there every day. Abraham had learned to walk and talk with God. Abraham had learned to depend on God and to live in faith.

We never can be sure what the end of life will bring. Illness, natural disaster, or even a major change in retirement income can happen to anyone. The one certain thing as we move forward is our God. He never tires of protecting His servants. He never tires of blessing His children. As we move forward with Him, the future is certain and even our last days can be full. We may not be rich, but we will have our daily bread. We may not be spry, but God will give us opportunity to use the skills and wisdom that He has invested in us throughout all our days. Last days should not be wasted days. It is a time to build on all that the Lord has given us in life. It is a time to try out dreams and new endeavors with the freedoms that retirement can bring. You are never too old to serve or to make a difference in the lives of others. God will be there and that will bring fullness to life.

- If you were free from having to make a living, what could you do that would bring the greatest impact on the people around you?

32. Faith's Advantage and Responsibility Hebrews 11: 8-19

Context: The author of the Hebrews writes over 2000 years after the death of Abraham about the legacy of this man of faith. His deeds are still well known today and are an encouragement to both Jew and Christian.

Good relationships are powerful. If you have a good working relationship with your boss, it makes it easier to get the resources and help you need to get assignments done. If you have a good relationship with your wife and children, family life will be a joy. Good relationships mean that you have people to help you and care for you. Good relationships also come with responsibilities. A single lie or complaint behind our boss's back can destroy that relationship. Adultery will poison a family for years. There are tremendous advantages to healthy relationships. It is up to us to do our part to maintain them. We have walked with Abraham and seen his faith relationship with the Lord. In the book of Hebrews, we see three ways that Abraham helped build that relationship throughout his life.

Abraham let the Lord choose where the relationship was going to happen. *"By faith Abraham, when called to go to a place he would later receive as his inheritance, obeyed and went, even though he did not know where he was going." (v.8)* Abraham trusted the Lord and followed God to a new place far from home. He became a stranger in this new land and prospered there because the Lord blessed him with great wealth and honor in this place. He learned to depend on the Lord in this strange place when there was no one else to lean on. God chose where He would bless Abraham. Abraham gave up the secure and familiar surroundings so that the Lord could make this new place a home for Abraham and an inheritance for his descendants.

Abraham had to let the Lord choose how the promises would be fulfilled. How happy he must have been when the Lord promised him that he would have descendants as numerous as the stars. He would not be the father of a family, but of a nation. Throughout his life, he wrestled at the timing of God's promise. *"By faith Abraham, even though he was past age--and Sarah herself was barren--was enabled to become a father because he considered him faithful who had made the promise." (v.11)* It would have been easier if the child had come at age 77 or 80, but God waited until Abraham was 100 years old. Abraham had to learn to trust God and His ways. God would bring the child when Abram had grown to be Abraham the patriarch. "How long?" was Abraham's cry. "When you are ready" was God's answer.

Abraham had to obey the Lord even when he did not understand why. God tested their relationship with a request that seems harsh. *"By faith Abraham, when God tested him, offered Isaac as a sacrifice. He who had received the promises was about to sacrifice his one and only son," (v.17)* Why God would want to take Isaac away was something that Abraham did not understand. God had said that Isaac was the son of promise. If Isaac died, how would the promises be fulfilled? The depth of their relationship and the trust that Abraham had in his Lord can be seen in the way that he obeyed when he didn't understand. The author of the Hebrews writes that Abraham figured God would do a miracle and raise Isaac from the dead.

Children of God who have a strong relationship with their God have an advantage over the rest of the world. Like Abraham, they have wisdom, protection and other blessings that come from a relationship with God. In the past devotions, we have seen how those blessings came to Abraham as he was responsible to God and obeyed his Lord. We also saw how failure to obey the Lord as he did in Egypt (Gen. 12) and in Gerar (Gen. 20) caused pain for Abraham and for those around him. One of the lessons of Abraham's life is that grace is freely given, but we also have a responsibility to live in that grace. The gifts of God are many, but we need to obey God even if we don't know why He is asking us to do something.

Faith is a relationship of great advantage. God called Abraham into that relationship and He calls you and me. Our God does not expect us to be perfect when we accept His gracious call. He does want us to follow so that He can shape and mold us as He did Abraham. As you ponder the journey that you have taken with Abraham, focus not on the wealth, the inherited land, or the fame. Focus on the faith relationship that Abraham had with the Lord and think about how that relationship gave him the strength, the courage and the support he needed to be the person that he became. God molded his life because Abraham was willing to trust and follow. The faith relationship with God was so precious that even Abraham's only son could be sacrificed to a God who would never let him down.

- What is the most important thing that you learned from your study of Abraham? How will you put that into action?

STUDENT WORKBOOK

(by corresponding devotion)

Bible Study: 2
God's Dreams for You Gen. 12: 2-9

From the moment that John held his new born son Patrick, he had dreams for his firstborn. He would play soccer like his dad and go to the best private schools. From there, he would go to college and study to be a doctor or an engineer so that he could change people's lives. Patrick would find a wonderful woman and raise a family near his parents so that they could share in all the joys of their grandchildren. Patrick was barely a few moments old and his father had a vision of what life could be.

The call of Abraham is about God's dreams for Abraham and is the pattern for God's plan for every Christian. God will mold Abraham into a man who will change the world through his faith. He will have so many children that they will become a great nation. God has such plans for you and for me if we will take time to listen to His words in the Bible and follow God all our lives. The life of Abraham shows that nothing is impossible for your future. Your Heavenly Father loves you and has great dreams for every one of you.

1. How do you feel when you first move to a new place?

2. God makes seven promises to Abram in verses 2 and 3. What conditions does God put on the promise?

3. How is Abraham a blessing to everyone that has or ever will live?

4. Which of Abram's promises would you most want and why? Would you want to be well known, be a blessing to others, have a great and strong family or have a place that you can call your own?

5. In following the Lord and leaving the prosperous city of Ur for the "wild west" of Palestine, what did Abraham lose and what did he gain?

6. If God made these promises to Abram in Ur of the Chaldeans as many think, where does Abram stop along the way and why only go half way?

7. Have you ever felt like God was calling you to trust Him and do something that others might not understand? What might hold you back from accepting the call?

8. Based on what you know of Abram, what has he done that makes him worthy of these promises?

9. What does Abram do when he gets to Bethel in the Promised Land? What does this action tell us about Abram's faith and direction in life?

10. What dreams might God have for you and how will you know where He is leading you?

This student guide may be copied for local church or small

group use. - taken from "32 days with Abraham" by Mark R.

Etter Copyright 2016

Bible Study: 6
Who controls your fate? Gen. 14:1-16

Amy fell into a group of kids that was nothing but trouble. They tipped over the principal's car, were regulars in after school detention and experimented with drugs. Her parents had lectured her and disciplined her, but nothing seemed to work. After she got arrested, they finally pulled her out of that high school and made sure that she was involved with new friends at her new school. It wasn't easy, but things slowly got better.

Lot had shared in Abram's blessings from God. His herds were so large that he could not share the same area with Abram and was given a choice of the hills above or the valley below. He chose the valley near Sodom. Soon he was living in Sodom and became one of the people of Sodom. It was a choice that he was destined to pay for. Like Lot, our fate is often controlled by the people around us. We need to carefully consider our friendships and our decisions. The choices that we make will affect our values and our future.

1. Describe your best friends in high school. Were they a good or bad influence on you?

2. Why mention this battle (v.1-12) in the bible? What does this have to do with the story of Abram?

3. What is the battle about (v.4)? Who wins the first battle (v.11)?

4. What slippery slope have we seen in the life of Lot as he leaves Abram and first tents near Sodom and then lives in Sodom? How does it impact his life (v.12)?

5. If Lot hadn't been living in Sodom, how much would the

battle have impacted Abram (v.13)? What does that say about his choices?

6. How do our choices in life reflect our values and character? How do they impact our outcome? What sort of values and considerations should guide our decision-making process?

7. How does Abram react to the news about Lot (v.13f)? Why do you think he reacted this way? Was it a good decision or a bad one?

8. How many men does Abram have to battle against the four armies of the east? What is the result of the battle?

9. What do you think the conversation was like between Abram and Lot on the way home from the battle? Did Lot's

time as a prisoner have any effect on him?

10. What is the lesson of this story for you?

Bible Study: 9
God Has Our Back - Gen. 15:8-19

"Mother, you promised! You promised that if I got my grades up, I could go to Purdue for college next year. Now you are telling me that I just have to go to the community college." "I am sorry, but we made that promise before your father got laid off of his job. If he gets a new job soon, we may be able to let you finish your last two years of school at Purdue." Judy stamped off to her bedroom and slammed the door. There are promises that we sometimes can't keep because life is beyond our control.

God had made remarkable promises to Abram in chapter 12. It was now years later and Abram wondered if the promises would come true. In an amazing display, God reaffirms those promises and gives Abram a vision of what will happen over the next 400 years. God keeps His promises for there is nothing that He can't do for Abram or for us. Trust Him, God has our back and our future in His hands.

1. What would someone have to do to convince you that a promise is true?

2. What question does Abram ask? (v.8) Looking at the context, what do you think caused him to bring up this question?

3. What does God command Abram to do? (v.9) What does Abram do with the animals and what does this mean?

4. During Abram's dream, God reveals the future. (v.13-16) What parts of the dream are comforting and what parts would be upsetting to Abram?

5. What does God specifically promise about Abram's life? (v.15)

6. If some offered to tell you what your future or the future of your children would be, would you want to know?

7. What is the torch and firepot passing between the rows of animals supposed to signify? (v.17)

8. How big is the promise that God makes to Abraham? (v.18-20) What must Abram do to receive this land for his descendants?

9. Share a time when God's blessings have exceeded what you might have reasonably expected.

10. Where in your life do you need some encouragement from God that He will keep His promises to you?

This student guide may be copied for local church or small

group use. - taken from "32 days with Abraham" by Mark R.

Etter Copyright 2016

Bible Study: 11
Submit to the Lord and Have Peace –
Gen. 16:4-16

When Don and Judy bought their first house, their two sons each eyed the corner bedroom and decided that it would belong to them. "I am the older child and so I get the larger bedroom", Bobby decreed. "I am Mommy's favorite and so I get the corner room" Billy replied. They pushed and shoved each other for a half hour only stopping when they noticed that both beds were going in the smaller hall bedroom. When they protested, their mother replied, "Your father and I have decided to make the corner bedroom into the guest room and study since we can't please you both.

Having come up with their own solution to the problem of an heir, Abram and Sarai face a major flaw in their logic. Hagar, the concubine, tries to take the role of mistress of the house since she is the mother of the new heir. Chaos ensues in the household. Finally, it is God who has to bring a temporary peace to this home. Hagar's lack of humility causes grief in this story and will ultimately force her out of the home.

By not controlling her pride, Hagar will eventually lose her

place.

1. When you were a kid, what kinds of things did you do that got you into trouble?

2. What did Abram and Sarai do that set up the conflict in this chapter? Does it make any difference that it was legal and commonly practiced in their day?

3. What are the viewpoints of each of the three main characters (Sarai, Abram, Hagar) in this argument about their status in the family? (v. 4-6)

4. What would be the Godly action for each of the three in this situation?

5. Of the three main characters, which do you think was most guilty for the split that was caused? Why?

6. What is Hagar's solution for the problem? What is shortsighted about that solution? (v. 6)

7. How do you handle conflict with others? Which of the three main characters do you emulate in dealing with conflict? Sarah (anger), Abraham (avoidance), or Hagar (fleeing)?

8. What does God command Hagar to do? Why is this the first part of the solution? What does God promise Hagar in return for her obedience? (v. 9)

9. How is Ishmael described by the Lord even before he is born? Why would his character make him an unsuitable person for God to have as the son of promise? (v. 12)

10. The Bible does not say, but how do you think Abram and Sarai treated Hagar when she came back after talking to the servant of the Lord?

Bible Study: 13
When God Calls You to Something New - Gen 17: 15-27

Jake looked at the baby in his arms. He and Jen had always wanted to be parents. Yet, there were adjustments when these new parents brought the baby home. First, they both had to get used to the 2 o'clock feedings and the diapers that smelled like rotting fish. They were a little sad when it became hard to have a meal out in a restaurant or even a quiet meal at home. Yet, as they held their little baby, they knew that this was one of the best times of their lives.

Abraham receives the great news that the promised son will be born within a year. With that news, he begins to wonder what it all will mean for Ishmael, the son he already has and loves. God promises to bless Ishmael but tells Abraham that the promises of greatness and land will belong to Isaac. God will not bless the child of the flesh, but only Isaac who is the child of the promise. The change will not be easy for Abraham, but God knows what is best.

1. What is the biggest change that you have ever made in your life? Did you plan to make the change or was the change something that life forced you to make?

2. What is the good change that is coming for Abraham? (v.17) How does Abraham receive the news?

3. What "bad" change does Abraham sense that the birth of Isaac will bring to his family? (v.18)

4. As you have made changes in your life, what "bad" things have come with the good?

5. How does God answer Abraham's request for Ishmael to receive the blessing? (v.19)

6. What does God promise about Ishmael in response to Abraham's plea? (v.20)

7. Why couldn't Ishmael be part of the blessing that was given to Isaac?

8. In what way was the birth of Isaac going to be a new era for Abraham? (v.22)

9. What was the point of circumcision? (v.23)

10. What changes do you need to make in your life right now? What would you lose and what blessings from the Lord could you gain by such a change?

Bible Study: 17
Learning God's Will - Gen. 18: 16-33

Tom had a great deal of talent as a carpenter, but he was often rash and in a hurry to start each project. Seeing him start on his latest project, his father said, "I hear you want to build a canoe here in the basement. How long do you think your canoe will be?" "Oh, I figure it will be about fifteen feet long when I get done", Tom replied. "Let me know when you get it done so we can figure out how to get it up the stairs" Looking at the narrow stairs out of the basement, "I guess I will build the pieces here and assemble it in the garage."

God could have just told Abraham what He was doing. None of us have the right to question God. Instead, God allowed a dialog so that Abraham could understand how evil Sodom and Gomorrah had become. God's love and respect for His patriarch are evident as Abraham comes to understand why such a loving God would feel compelled to destroy the cities of the plain. Given the chance, I believe that God still would rather teach us in prayer so that we understand not only what God is doing, but also why.

1. What is one thing that you would like God to explain to you?

2. How does God describe the relationship that He has with Abraham? (v. 18-19) What purpose does God already have in mind for Abraham?

3. How might it have affected the relationship between Abraham and God if God had destroyed Sodom without talking to Abraham? Has God ever given you a premonition of something before it happened?

4. How will God determine what He will do next? (v.20-21) Do you think that God already has in mind what He will do? If so, why send the angels to Sodom?

5. Abraham is horrified at the prospect of destroying the cities. What does he appeal to as he talks with God (v.25)? Why

can't Abraham appeal based on Sodom's worth or the relationship he has with God?

6. How does Abraham see his own personal worth (v.27)? What do you think gives him the courage to talk to God?

7. Does Abraham change God's mind (v.32)? What does Abraham learn from this discussion? How would the discussion help Abraham see the wisdom of God?

8. How does God show His love and patience for Abraham? How has God shown His love and patience with you in your life?

9. Abraham intercedes for a wicked people. Do you think that was pleasing to God? What does it show about Abraham?

10 What would you most like to emulate about Abraham in this story?

This student guide may be copied for a local church or small group use. - taken from "32 days with Abraham" by Mark R. Etter Copyright 2016

Bible study: 18
Be Careful What You Wish For –
Gen. 19:1-29

John had always dreamed of having a BMW. Now a shiny new "Beemer" sat on his driveway and he would be the envy of all his friends. That feeling of elation lasted for about a week. In the mail, he got a bill showing exactly what his insurance was going to cost. Three months later, he slid on some ice and "bumped" a light pole. He almost had heart failure when he saw what the repair would cost. He started looking for a simpler car before his dream became a nightmare. The BMW was a lot of fun, but he just couldn't afford this dream.

Lot had been enamored with Sodom for years. He had gladly chosen the valley as his portion from Abram and soon moved into the city and become an official of the city. Yet the dream turned into a nightmare that cost Lot everything. He loses his possessions, his morals, and even his wife. Dazzled by the "glitter" of Sodom, he hadn't counted the cost of its evil ways. All of us need to be careful what we wish for. The

dream we so desire may not be what it first seems.

1. Where have you visited that was so beautiful or exciting that you would move there tomorrow if you had a chance?

2. Who comes to visit Lot and where do they find him? (v.1)

3. When the visitors announce that they will just spend the night in the square, why does Lot offer lodging? (v.2-3)

4. How do the men of the city show their true character once it becomes dark? (v.4-5) What surprising offer does Lot make to save the visitors? (v.8)

5. What qualities of people should be an immediate sign that these are people that you need to limit your exposure with?

6. What do the two visitors do when Lot's life seems to be in danger? (v.10-11) Why should this have been a sign for Lot to take these two men seriously?

7. How did the message given to Lot (v.12-13) contrast with the message that had just been given to Abraham up in the hills?

8. Why was Lot hesitant to leave the city? (v.16)

9. Why is it so hard to leave behind things that we know are bad for us?

10. As you look at the story of Lot in Sodom, what were the consequences of living in Sodom for Lot?

Bible Study: 20
Even Saints Sin - Gen. 20:1-18

Bill sat and looked at the bars on his jail cell. "How could I have been so stupid?" He had been shoplifting at the local convenience store with some buddies and he had been the one who had gotten caught. He had been allowed to call his father in order to make bail but had a lump in his throat when his father appeared. He started to cry and blurted out how sorry he was. He was afraid his father would lecture him but was surprised when he received a hug. "You messed up, but I'll stand with you and help you through this."

The bible never tries to cover up the fact that Abraham sinned. In this text, he lied and someone else paid the price. Yet, God stood with His patriarch. He protected Sarah and bailed Abraham out of an ugly mess once he admitted what he had done. God never condones sin, but He never abandons us when we sin. He is always willing to redeem and restore the repentant sinner. When we sin, it is always better to go to the Lord for help rather than try to save ourselves.

1. Name one mistake that you have done at least twice. How did you handle the consequences of the mistake?

2. What did Abraham say about Sarah? Why do you think that he made this mistake a second time? (v.2)

3. What happens because of Abraham's lie? What and whom does Abraham put in jeopardy?

4. How have you seen lies impact people around you?

5. How does Abimelech's dream show God's concern for all the people involved? (v.3)

6. Ironically, who is paying the penalty for Abraham's sin? Why did God inflict this penalty?

7. In what ways do we often make others suffer to protect ourselves or hide from our sins?

8. What is God's command to Abimelech? (v.7) Why do you think that God speaks so clearly to this pagan king?

9. How does Abraham try to explain his way out of trouble? (v.11)

10. Why do you think that God didn't give up on Abraham at this point? How does that show God can be merciful to His people when they still sin against Him?

This student guide may be copied for a local church or small group use. - taken from "32 days with Abraham" by Mark R. Etter Copyright 2016

Bible Study: 23
Difficult Choices - Genesis 21: 8-21

Jane, Bob's old flame from high school moved back to town. Bob had a lot of good times with Jane before she went off to Michigan State. Now she has invited Bob out on a date and he is wondering what to do. The problem is that he has been out on a few dates with Sue. It is nothing serious, but he doesn't want to lose Sue if the evening with Jane can't rekindle what they once had. He likes both women and realizes that if he is not careful he will lose them both.

Abraham has two sons and two women who are both vying to be the leader of the household. It would be nice if they could all get along and live as one happy family, but that is obviously not going to happen. He must make a choice when Sarah puts her foot down and tells him that Hagar and Ishmael must go. God helps His servant with that choice by laying out what is at stake and by promising to bless both sons because of His love for Abraham.

1. What motivates you to make the hard decisions like taking a new job or breaking up with a friend?

2. What triggers the problem in the house of Abraham? (v.8) How has a good thing created a big problem?

3. From Sarah's perspective, why must Hagar and Ishmael be sent away? (v10) What do you think that she fears?

4. Who, like Sarah, do you find it hard to get along with? How do you handle it? Is there something you can do to make things better?

5. What is at the heart of Abraham's distress? (v.11)

6. How would you feel if you had to send your son away?

7. What wisdom does God share with Abraham? (v.12) What reason does God give for making this hard choice?

8. While Ishmael was outside of God's covenant and promise, what assurances does God give to Hagar about her son? (v.18) Why would God bless this troublesome teen?

9. In choosing Isaac over Ishmael, was God being fair?

10. What difficult choices have you faced or are you facing right now? What does the example of Abraham show you about trusting the Lord's direction in those decisions?

Bible Study: 26
Entrusting Your Children to God - Gen. 22:1-19

John had known Tom for close to twenty years, but he still felt more than a little apprehensive. Tom was going to a remote village in Guatemala on a church mission trip and had invited four high school youth to come along including John's daughter Karen. John trusted Tom, but there were so many things that could happen. Karen could get hurt or even die in some accident far from a decent hospital. Saying good-bye as Karen left the waiting area for her airplane was one of the hardest things John had ever done.

Abraham's life was bound up in his son Isaac. Now God was telling Abraham to sacrifice his son to show that Abraham loved God more than Isaac. How that must have torn this man of faith apart. How could the promises God had made to Abraham be kept if Isaac was dead? In one of the greatest acts of faith in the Bible, Abraham obeyed the Lord. In the end, Isaac was not killed, but Abraham and Isaac saw the depth of God's love for them and learned that they could trust the Lord for the rest of their lives.

1. What possession or person would be hardest for you to give up?

2. What command does God give to Abraham in verse 2? What is at stake for Abraham if Isaac dies?

3. How does Abraham respond to this command? (v.3)

4. What do you picture Abraham thinking as he hears and responds to this command? How would you feel if you were asked you to give up something precious to you?

5. How far away is Moriah (v.4)? How would this make the test more difficult?

6. Many think that Isaac is a teenager at the time of the test. What question does he ask (v.7) and how does Abraham answer (v.8)?

7. On the mountain, how does Abraham show the depth of his faith? (v.10) Do you think that Abraham would have really killed his son?

8. When does God stop the sacrifice (v.11) and what can we learn from God's timing?

9. How does God provide the sacrifice as Abraham said he would (v.13)?

10 What does Abraham's example teach us about trusting the Lord enough to obey Him in every situation?

Bible Study: 30
Knowing When to Say Yes - Gen. 24:15-67

The job offer came out of nowhere. A headhunter from Cincinnati called and told Tom that he was being considered to head a new division of Proctor and Gamble. Would he be willing to fly at company expense for a job interview? He was immediately interested and flew out the next week. After the second interview, he was offered the dream job. The answer was easy because Mary, his wife, and he had been weighing the pros and cons and praying about this opportunity throughout the process. He immediately said yes and prepared for one of the biggest changes in his life.

Rebekah receives the offer to marry and must decide within 24 hours if she will accept. Showered with gold and silver jewelry, she has the offer of a lifetime. She can become the wife of Isaac who is heir to a vast fortune, but it will mean moving from her family. Sensing the opportunity, her family leaves the decision to her, but she already knows what her decision will be. Her confidence brings her into the family of Abraham and makes her an ancestor of Jesus Christ.

1. How do you know when to say yes to a decision?

2. What problems would have been created if Isaac had married a Canaanite? How does marrying a relative negate those problems?

3. What sign does the servant ask from the Lord? (v.14) How does this show the servant's trust in the Lord and his willingness to allow the Lord to make the choice?

 4. Others ask for signs in scripture like Gideon in the book of Judges. What sign might you ask for if you were ill or if you were asked to take over a ministry at church?

5. How did Rebekah react when she saw the need of the stranger? (v.19) How do the qualities that she exhibits show that she is an exceptional young woman?

6. If you ask for a sign, how might you know that it is a sign from God and not from another source?

7. How does the family react to this proposal from Abraham through his servant? (v.55)

8. What is Rebekah's answer when the servant is in a hurry to have an answer and return to Palestine? (v.58) What do you think led her to this answer?

9. What was at stake in her answer? What would the rest of the Bible look like if she had said no?

10. What have you learned about difficult decisions?

Bible Study: 31
Full of Years - Gen. 25:1-19

Mary was 94 years old on the afternoon that she died from a heart attack. She had lived without Harold, her husband, for 25 years but had been active and relatively healthy up to the end. She was never rich, but she died in her own home with several of her children by her side as they waited for the ambulance. Her last words were to remind them that she would see each of them in heaven. When she heard the siren of the ambulance in front of her house, she knew it was time to go and asked the Lord to take her home.

Having passed the torch of promise to Isaac, the Bible story seems to forget about Abraham for a while. Suddenly, we read about the death of Abraham at the age of 175. We can only guess what life was like after the death of Sarah thirty-eight years before. Yet, these few verses describe a man who died "full of years" and with a quality of life that most people would envy. Those thirty-eight years were not empty but filled with a second wife and six more children. God blessed him to the end. His walk with the Lord brought joy and fulfillment.

1. What is your dream for your retirement years?

2. Abraham was 137 years old when Sarah died. How did Abraham live his life after the death of Sarah? (v.1)

3. With the six other children, Abraham had eight children with three women. How is his estate divided (v.5) Why is this division?

4. What happened to Keturah's children? What might Abraham be afraid of?

5. How is the life of Abraham described in verse 8? How is that a great compliment to this patriarch?

6. How would you like your life to be described at your death? What characteristics do you think are most important?

7. What do you think made Abraham's life a success? How will that influence how you live?

8. Where is Abraham buried? (v.9)

9. What do you admire most about the life of Abraham? What would you like to emulate in your life?

LEADER'S GUIDE

(by corresponding devotion)

2 God's Dreams for You - Gen. 12:2-9

1. How do you feel when you first move to a new place?

Answers will vary but may range from scared and lost to excited and happy. Let them share how the move was good or bad for them as well.

2. God makes seven promises to Abram in verses 2 and 3. What conditions does God put on the promise?

The seven promises are: "I will make you a great nation." "I will bless you." "I will make your name great." "You shall be a blessing." "I will bless those who bless you." "The one who curses you I will curse." "And in you all the families of the earth will be blessed." God makes no conditions on the promises. God said, "I will." God will make Abraham's name great and will bless the whole world through him and through his descendent, Jesus Christ.

3. How is Abraham a blessing to everyone that has or ever will live?

Surely, every American could say that we are blessed by the work of Washington or Lincoln. Yet, few in Africa or Asia could say that they were blessed by these men. Through Jesus who is the descendant of Abram, everyone in the world has been blessed. The death and resurrection of Jesus changes the possible future of every living person. God will take this ordinary man and make him the beginning of a movement that will change the history of the world. Abram's faith and life will inspire many and be an example that many will follow.

4. Which of Abram's promises would you most want and why? Would you want to be well known, be a blessing to others, have a great and strong family or have a place that you can call your own?

Answers will vary but let them think about the scope of the promises and the joy that they would have if even one of these promises was fulfilled.

5. In following the Lord and leaving the prosperous city of Ur for the "wild west" of Palestine, what did Abraham lose and what did he gain?

Ur was a great and prosperous city. Archaeology has shown that the city was a great civilization. Canaan was more like the American West with few comforts and conveniences. Abram and Sarai gave up the luxury of Ur to follow God's command. Yet the Lord promises that as much as Abram has lost, his descendants will gain even more. *"To your offspring, I will give this land."(v. 7)* He has left a city, he will gain a country and a home. He has left the prosperity of Ur, but he will have great wealth and honor in this new place. All that Abram has left, the Lord will fill with new blessings. His willingness to follow God would open the door for the Lord to bless him in ways that he never imagined.

6. If God made these promises to Abram in Ur of the Chaldeans as many think, where does Abram stop along the way and why only go half way?

The first steps of faith are not always giant steps, which may explain why Abraham did not fully obey God. Instead of leaving his family (Gen. 12:1), as he was commanded, Abraham took his father and his nephew Lot with him when he left Ur; and then he stayed at Haran until his father died. It may have been a son's love for his aged father that made Abraham stop in Haran (Gen. 11:31) until the death of his father (?), but Abram does finally set out from Haran at the age of 75 (Genesis 12:4).

7. Have you ever felt like God was calling you to trust Him and do something that others might not understand? What might hold you back from accepting the call?

Answers will vary, but panic, uncertainty, and feeling not up to the task are all fears that inhibit us from doing great things.

8. Based on what you know of Abram, what has he done that makes him worthy of these promises?

The man from Ur seems average at best. One of the challenges for us is that little is said of Abram before these promises and what the Bible says of his early life is time filled with a lot of mistakes. Today, Abraham is a person that Jews, Christians and Muslims all think about as their father. He is a model and life example for all of us. As we first meet him, Abram is not yet that man. God will mold His servant and give him character. God will bless the foreigner and make him someone that his neighbors consider a mighty prince (Gen. 23:5). God will do for Abram and for us what no man can do for themselves. He will make us great by changing our character and our future.

9. What does Abram do when he gets to Bethel in the Promised Land? What does this action tell us about Abram's faith and direction in life?

Abram builds an altar and calls on the name of the Lord. It would become a mark of Abram that he was a man known for his tent and his altar. The tent marked him as a pilgrim who had not yet inherited the land where he lived. The altar marked him as a man of God who was devoted to the Lord. Sadly, whenever Abram abandoned his tent and altar (Gen. 12:10-20), he found himself in trouble for forgetting his God.

10. What dreams might God have for you and how will you know where He is leading you?

Encourage them to dream big. God can do great things in our lives and let us be someone who changes the lives of many by the power of the Lord. How will you know the dreams are true? We have the advantage of the counsel of our fellow Christians and the Bible to tell us what is right and what matches the person that God made in us.

6 Who controls your fate? - Gen. 14:1-16

1. Describe your best friends in high school. Was they a good or bad influence on you?

Answers will vary. People deny it but your friends determine your fate. If you don't believe it, look at your kids. The friends that your children choose determine their future. Let a child get in with the wrong group and you will have nothing but trouble.

2. Why mention this battle (v.1-12) in the bible? What does this have to do with the story of Abram?

This reason this first battle is mentioned in the Bible becomes clear as the rest of the story unfolds. Lot lives in Sodom and is taken as a prisoner. Abram will defy the odds and wage war to redeem his nephew Lot. .

3. What is the battle about (v.4)? Who wins the first battle (v.11)?

The five cities of the plains rebel against their masters, the four cities of the east. The armies from the east march out to wage war on the rebellious cities of the plains. In response, *"the king of Sodom . . . marched out and drew up their battle lines." (v.8)* One would have expected that the five cities could defend themselves on their own turf, but they are routed and many fall into tar pits in the midst of their escape. The conquering army takes the goods and people of Sodom and Gomorrah as they depart.

4. What slippery slope have we seen in the life of Lot as he leaves Abram and first tents near Sodom and then lives in Sodom? How does it impact his life (v.12)?

Lot had moved from outside the city (13:12) to be in the city

(14:12). Now he would share their fate. Nothing in the text says that he went out into the battle, but *"They also carried off Abram's nephew Lot and his possessions." (v.12)* He would pay the price for their loss because he had now become one of them. Perhaps, he felt that he could separate himself from their evil and live among them, but not really become one of them. Whatever his thoughts, he had thrown his portion in with Sodom and now was reaping the fruit of his choices. The capture of Lot demonstrates that you will share the fate of those whom you call friends.

5. If Lot hadn't been living in Sodom, how much would the battle have impacted Abram (v.13)? What does that say about his choices?

Abraham lived up in the high country and did not get involved in the war until he heard that Lot had been captured. He was separate from Sodom and Gomorrah, but he was not isolated from the people around him. Abram had made alliances with some of the local leaders in the hill country who went into battle with him (Gen 14:24). Abram had chosen to live in the hills with the Lord and not in sinful cities of the valley (Gen 18:16f).

6. How do our choices in life reflect our values and character? How do they impact our outcome? What sort of values and considerations should guide our decision-making process?

Answers may include the fact that adults who frequent the bars or hang around with people who have trouble holding down a job will be pulled down by their friends. Adults who spend a lot of time around strong Christians or have a set of friends with strong morals will be pulled up by these friends. Let them discuss the consequences of their friendships.

7. How does Abram react to the news about Lot (v.13f)? Why do you think he reacted this way? Was it a good decision or a bad one?

News came to Abram that his nephew had been captured and was being taken by the four kings of the east as bounty. Compassion welled up in him and he felt that he had to rescue his wayward nephew. Abram had stayed away from the battle because he was an outsider. He was separate from the politics and intrigue of the world around him. Yet, now that Lot's life was on the line, he felt compelled to act even though Lot had acted foolishly. He was willing to do something to help his nephew and others overcome the danger that they now found themselves in. He was separated from the world, but that didn't mean that he was uncaring or indifferent.

8. How many men does Abram have to battle against the four armies of the east? What is the result of the battle?

Abram has 318 trained men in his household which speaks of how extensive his flocks had become. Abraham and his allies chased the enemy for 100 miles, freed all the captives, and recovered all the spoils. This was a mighty victory that Abram recognizes was a gift of God (Gen. 14:20)

9. What do you think the conversation was like between Abram and Lot on the way home from the battle? Did Lot's time as a prisoner have any effect on him?

The Bible doesn't tell us of the conversation but have the class dream what such a conversation would sound like. Sadly, neither the Lord's chastening nor the Lord's goodness in rescuing Lot did him any good. One might have expected him to repent, but he returned to Sodom and later lost it all (Gen.19)

10. What is the lesson of this story for you?

Answers may vary but see if the group can come up with two or three applications concerning choices, friends, and helping others.

9 God Has Our Back - Gen. 15:8-19

1. What would someone have to do to convince you that a promise is true?

Answers will vary and may include putting it in writing or swearing before a third party. There may even be people that we may never believe no matter what they do.

2. What question does Abram ask? (v.8) Looking at the context, what do you think caused him to bring up this question?

Abram asks how he can know that he will gain possession of the land. Abram's question to God is in response to God's renewed promise that the Lord would belong to Abram's descendants. He may have wondered whether the land would belong to his descendants for long since he just watched nine nations battle for this piece of land. It was one thing for Abram to own the land. How would he know that his descendants would keep it?

3. What does God command Abram to do? (v.9) What does Abram do with the animals and what does this mean?

What is described in verses 9-17 was known in Abram's day as "cutting a covenant." Two people would make a treaty involving the death of animals and the binding of people to a promise. The persons making the covenant would sacrifice animals and divide the bodies, placing half of each animal across from the other half on the ground. The two parties would walk between the pieces of the sacrifices declaring that they deserved to be cut in two if either of them did not keep the covenant. (See Jer. 34:18-19.)

4. During Abram's dream, God reveals the future. (v.13-16)

What parts of the dream are comforting and what parts would be upsetting to Abram?

Much of the books of Genesis and Exodus are laid out before Abram. The trip to Egypt rescuing them from the famine, their slavery under the Egyptians and their rescue in the days of Moses are all laid out. It surely would be unsettling to think of your descendants in slavery, but nice to know that God will bring them back and give them this land.

5. What does God specifically promise about Abram's life? (v.15)

God promised Abram would live to a good old age. This is fulfilled when Abram lived to be 175 years old and never saw any of the pain that his descendants would experience. (Gen. 25:7) God gave Abram a century of life after the promises were first given and 75 years with his son Isaac.

6. If some offered to tell you what your future or the future of your children would be, would you want to know?

Answers will vary, but this question may help people understand how Abram might have felt about this vision of the future.

7. What is the torch and firepot passing between the rows of animals supposed to signify? (v.17)

The torch is the presence of God. He alone passes through the rows of animals and not Abram. God is making a promise about the future. The covenant is one sided. God will keep the covenant and fulfill the promises that He made. Abram is promised a gift with no requirements.

8. How big is the promise that God makes to Abraham? (v.18-20) What must Abram do to receive this land for his descendants?

While Abraham must have been hoping for the area of

Palestine where he was raising sheep, the area described by God is a vast area. Only in the time of David and Solomon would the Jews control an area this big. You will notice that the promise is based only on God's mercy. God again makes no requirements on Abram to receive the land.

9. Share a time when God's blessings have exceeded what you might have reasonably expected.

This question may be hard for some in the group. Give them time to think back on their life and see the blessings of the Lord on their lives. The focus of the question is on the generosity of God's gifts.

10. Where in your life do you need some encouragement from God that He will keep His promises to you?

Answers will vary. If it seems appropriate, take some time and pray about some of the areas mentioned. Let the power of prayer help anyone who is struggling.

11 Submit to the Lord and have peace - Gen. 16:4-16

1. When you were a kid, what kinds of things did you do that got you into trouble?

You will find a variety of answers. Give people a chance to share their stories as a way of getting to know each other better and understand the consequences of sin.

2. What did Abram and Sarai do that set up the conflict in this chapter? Does it make any difference that it was legal and commonly practiced in their day?

God had promised a son many years before, but that child had not come. Sarai hatched a plan that would solve their dilemma. Up till now, the Bible does not record that God had promised that Sarai was to be the mother of the peoples as numerous as the stars. The promises were all to Abram. She makes the sacrifice and takes *'her Egyptian maid servant Hagar and gave her to her husband to be his wife." (v.3)*. She thought that Hagar would bear the child to fulfill the promises. All the promises that God had made to Abram could now come true. This child would inherit the land and would make Abram's name great.

3. What are the viewpoints of each of the three main characters (Sarai, Abram, Hagar) in this argument about their status in the family? (v. 4-6)

Her plan has unintended consequences. The maid who has now become the second "wife" has an attitude. *"When she knew she was pregnant, she began to despise her mistress." (v.4)* As the mother of the heir, Hagar felt like she deserved special treatment. She, not Sarai, would be the mistress of the household. Sarai, however, would not tolerate such feelings and pushed back. She was not about to be second rate behind an Egyptian slave. Abraham seems to feel that they should just get along. He shirks his duty and gives the problem right back to Sarai. *"Your servant is in your hands, do with her whatever you think best." (v.6)* The servant is hers and as mistress of the household, Sarai should be able to deal with her servants. He fails his wife. He fails his child that Hagar is carrying. He even fails to act as the master of the house and settle a dispute in his family.

4. What would be the Godly action for each of the three in this situation?

Answers may vary, but perhaps the first thing they should have done was build an altar, worship the Lord, and tell Him their problems. They should have confessed their sins and received His gracious forgiveness. Once you stop fighting with God and with yourself, you will have an easier time not fighting with others. The first step toward reconciliation with others is getting right with God.

5. Of the three main characters, which do you think was most guilty for the split that was caused? Why?

Each of the three characters shares blame for the problem. Let the class discuss how each reacted badly. You might have fun voting for the guiltiest party.

6. What is Hagar's solution for the problem? What is shortsighted about that solution? (v. 6)

Hagar's solution was to *run away from the problem,* a tactic common to man since Adam and Eve (Gen. 3:8). However, you soon discover that you cannot solve problems by running away. Abraham learned that when he fled to Egypt (12:10ff). There was peace in the home for a short time, but it was not the "peace of God."

7. How do you handle conflict with others? Which of the three main characters do you emulate in dealing with conflict? Sarah (anger), Abraham (avoidance), or

Hagar (fleeing)?

Answers will vary, but this can be a good opportunity to see the flaws in each of the three strategies and look for better solutions for class members.

8. What does God command Hagar to do? Why is this the first part of the solution? What does God promise Hagar in return for her obedience? (v. 9)

The Lord sees the misery of this family and steps in. The angel of the Lord tells Hagar. *"Go back to your mistress and submit to her." (v.9)* She cannot run from the problem that she helped create. Because of His love for Abram and for the child, God promises that the child will have *"descendants too numerous to count." (v.10)* God's intervention brings some peace to the family. God's intervention reminds us that God is concerned with our pain, even when it is self-inflicted. As we listen to Him, peace can come.

9. How is Ishmael described by the Lord even before he is born? Why would his character make him an unsuitable person for God to have as the son of promise? (v. 12)

The description of Ishmael is not very flattering. He would be a "wild donkey of a man" (16:12,), who lives in the wilderness and survives by his skill as an archer. He will be independent and will be hated as he lives "in hostility toward all his brothers" (Gen. 16:12). His descendants, the Arab nations, are also independent peoples who dwell in the desert lands and resist the encroachments of other nations.

10. The Bible does not say, but how do you think Abram and Sarai treated Hagar when she came back after talking to the servant of the Lord?

Surely, the fact that God spoke directly to Hagar would have forced Abraham and Sarah to change and to learn to live with their mistakes. The Bible tells us that Abraham's heart was full of love for Ishmael (17:18) and peace seemed to exist in the house until Isaac is born and Ishmael feels threatened (21:1-11).

13 When God Calls You to Something New - Genesis 17: 15-27

1. What is the biggest change that you have ever made in your life? Did you plan to make the change or was the change something that life forced you to make?

Answers will vary. Changes come to us, either by plan or by force. As the group discusses changes they had to make, they will feel some of the angst that Abraham felt about this change that God was making in his life.

2. What is the good change that is coming for Abraham? (v.17) How does Abraham receive the news?

The good news is simply that the time has come for God to fulfill His promise of a son for Abraham. In reaction, Abraham laughs. There are three different times when laughter is connected with Isaac's birth. Here, Abraham laughed for joy when he heard Sarah would have a son. Later Sarah laughed in unbelief when God told her the news (18:9-15). Finally, Sarah laughed for joy when Isaac was born (21:6-7). The name Isaac means "he laughs."

3. What "bad" change does Abraham sense that the birth of Isaac will bring to his family? (v.18)

Abraham wonders what place his son, Ishmael, has in God's plan. We can't blame Abraham for interceding for Ishmael. Ishmael was his son whom he loved. He had watched Ishmael grow up for thirteen years and wondered what the future was for this young man entering adulthood.

4. As you have made changes in your life, what "bad"

things have come with the good?

Answers may vary, but may include leaving friends when we moved for a new job or having little time for ourselves when the Lord blessed us with children. Change can often bring loss.

5. How does God answer Abraham's request for Ishmael to receive the blessing? (v.19)

God affirms that the blessings promised in Genesis 12 are reserved for Isaac. Ishmael was the son of the flesh conceived when Abram and Sarai had doubts about God's promise. Isaac would be the miracle son in their old age who would be the blessing that God had promised to Abraham and the carrier of all the promises that God made. Just as the covenant was given to Abraham, God would make the same covenant with Isaac and bless the world through him.

6. What does God promise about Ishmael in response to Abraham's plea? (v.20)

God promises that He has heard Abraham and will make the descendants of Ishmael numerous. He too will be a great nation with twelve princes coming from his family. He will not be discarded but will be blessed greatly by the Lord for the sake of Abraham.

7. Why couldn't Ishmael be part of the blessing that was given to Isaac?

The two brothers could not coexist in the same home. God knew that Ishmael would bring dissension into the home (Gen 21:8f) and Isaac would bring laughter. Abraham had to let Ishmael go if Isaac was to flourish. When God is preparing a bright future for us, we cannot cling to the things of the past. Often those things will get in the way of the blessings that God has planned for us. We must be ready to give up the things that seem so good for something better that God has in mind for us.

8. In what way was the birth of Isaac going to be a new era for Abraham? (v.22)

Abraham had finally matured into the man that God wanted. The old Abram took things into his own hands because he struggled with the promise. The new Abraham would have the promise in a son and be willing to sacrifice his son rather than losing his God. The promises were to become real for Abraham as God made them flesh and blood in Isaac. It was God's way of showing that all the other promises that He had made would come true as well.

9. What was the point of circumcision? (v.23)

Circumcision was the badge of the covenant. God had made a promise to Abraham and to his descendants. Circumcision was a reminder of that covenant and a commitment from the people to live their lives in faith with their God. It was a badge of honor showing that they were different from the rest of the world. It was also a good work that showed that believed in God and would dedicate themselves to Him.

10. What changes do you need to make in your life right now? What would you lose and what blessings from the Lord could you gain by such a change?

Answers will vary but may focus on sins that need to be put behind them or ministry that the Lord may be asking them to do. Both will have some loss but will also have tremendous gains as we obey and follow the Lord with our lives.

17 Learning God's Will - Gen. 18: 16-33

1. What is one thing that you would like God to explain to you?

The question may elicit a variety of answers. Give people a chance to share their burning questions with God but keep this question from going too long.

2. How does God describe the relationship that He has with Abraham? (v.18-19) What purpose does God already have in mind for Abraham?

Abraham is given the title of "friend" in 2 Chron. 20:7, Isaiah 41:8, and James 2:23. The text demonstrates the friendship that God feels for Abraham. God gives two reasons for revealing His plans to Abraham. Abraham will become a great nation who will bless the world. Second, God chose Abraham to establish a people who would keep the way of the Lord. God has great plans for Abraham and this is an opportunity to teach the patriarch something that will impact people for generations.

3. How might it have affected the relationship between Abraham and God if God had destroyed Sodom without talking to Abraham? Has God ever given you a premonition of something before it happened?

God could have destroyed the city without ever setting foot on earth, but He took the time to teach. If God had destroyed the two cities including Lot and his family, Abraham might have wondered about the justice of God. God uses this dialog to teach Abraham that not even 10 righteous people live in Sodom and that a just God must deal with evil. Their answers may vary on the premonition. Be sure to ask them what made them think that God was talking to them at this time.

4. How will God determine what He will do next? (v.20-21) Do you think that God already has in mind what He will do? If so, why send the angels to Sodom?

The Lord would send the angels to investigate Sodom and Gomorrah for two reasons: the outcry coming from their victims was immense, and the cities' sin was extremely serious. God is all knowing, but Abraham needs to see God's concern for the people of Sodom. A visual inspection will help Abraham understand that God's punishment was not arbitrary, but rather the cry that came up to God was justified. The angels will also be able to rescue Lot.

5. Abraham is horrified at the prospect of destroying the cities. What does he appeal to as he talks with God (v.25)? Why can't Abraham appeal have based on Sodom's worth or the relationship he has with God?

What is amazing is that he never shies from speaking the question on his mind. He knows that the Lord will not destroy him or get angry with him for an honest question. Abraham bases his questions for God on the knowledge that God is just and merciful. Abraham's prayer was based not on the mercy of God but on the justice of God. A just and holy God could not destroy righteous believers with wicked unbelievers. He seems to hope that Sodom has enough righteous people, but he is not confident of that fact.

6. How does Abraham see his own personal worth (v.27)? What do you think gives him the courage to talk to God?

He speaks to God with deep humility and with the knowledge that it is blessing to have a God who is patient and willing to listen. He doesn't beg God to do anything. He doesn't claim that God can't destroy the city or claim that the city is not evil. He simply wants to understand why God is doing what He is doing. Abraham may have been convinced that there were at least ten believers in the city. Lot and his extended family alone would have been far more than ten people.

7. Does Abraham change God's mind (v.32)? What does Abraham learn from this discussion? How would the discussion help Abraham see the wisdom of God?

God still destroyed Sodom and Gomorrah, but He did rescue Lot and two of his daughters from Sodom. It is Abraham whose mind is changed. He saw that God was merciful and would not "sweep the righteous away with the wicked" in Sodom. Sadly, there were few righteous in Sodom. Abraham sees that God has no pleasure in the death of the wicked (Ezek. 33:11), but that God must be just and protect His world from evil.

8. How does God show His love and patience for Abraham? How has God shown His love and patience with you in your life?

He could have destroyed the city in a moment, but He took the time to teach. God uses dialog to teach Abraham the depth of the evil in Sodom and the importance of people to God. As few as ten people would have saved a whole city from destruction! Lot could have saved the city if even ten of his family and those who worked for him were righteous. God doesn't argue with Abraham. He listens and lets Abraham learn of the situation in Sodom. Answers will vary about their personal experience. Stress that God is eager to have such times of teaching with us.

9. Abraham intercedes for a wicked people. Do you think that was pleasing to God? What does it show about Abraham?

Abraham shows that he has the heart of God as he did not want to see all those people perish. He had kept himself separate from them after the battle (Gen. 14:22-24), but here he shows that he still cares about them. God surely is happy when we care about everyone in our world including the sinners around us.

**10 What would you most like to emulate about Abraham
in this story?**

Answers will vary, but might include his heart for others, his
ability to talk to God, or his willingness to accept God's will.

18 Be Careful What You Wish For - Gen. 19:1-29

1. Where have you visited that was so beautiful or exciting that you would move there tomorrow if you had a chance?

Answers will vary. It may be an exciting city that they really enjoyed on a visit or a beautiful place in the Rocky Mountains or on the beach. Explore why this is a special place and what consequences there might be for moving.

2. Who comes to visit Lot and where do they find him? (v.1)

The "men" sent by God have come to Sodom and find Lot sitting in the gateway of the city. Lot found the area of Sodom desirable (Gen. 13:10-11). Then he moved his tent near Sodom (v.12), and finally, he moved into Sodom (14:12). Lot's location in the gate indicates that he was a man of some authority in the city, for that was where official business was conducted (Ruth 4:1). He was no longer an outsider, he had truly become one of this wicked city.

3. When the visitors announce that they will just spend the night in the square, why does Lot offer lodging? (v.2-3)

The visitors arrive in the evening, perhaps just before dusk. Lot insists that they spend the night with him because he knows what will happen to them if they camp out in the square. To his credit, Lot prepares them a meal and gives them a place to sleep. He shows hospitality for his visitors even if it is not as great as Abraham had done (Gen. 18:1-8)

4. How do the men of the city show their true character

once it becomes dark? (v.4-5) What surprising offer does Lot make to save the visitors? (v.8)

The men of Sodom want Lot to hand over the visitors "so that we can have sex with them". (v.5) This is such a violation of God's rules and the rules of hospitality that even Lot is taken back when they say it. (v.6) Lot's values have suffered in Sodom. He offers his two virgin daughters to the crowd in order to save the visitors. One wonders what the daughters thought of the bargain.

5. What qualities of people should be an immediate sign that these are people that you need to limit your exposure with?

Answers will vary but may include someone who gets angry or blames others, someone who lies or swindles others to make himself look good, or someone who is willing to cheat on his wife or tells dirty jokes. We should witness to them but need to be careful around them because all of these people are ones who could bring you down with them.

6. What do the two visitors do when Lot's life seems to be in danger? (v.10-11) Why should this have been a sign for Lot to take these two men seriously?

The angels reach out and grab Lot back into the house and blind the men of Sodom so that Lot is safe for the moment. The miracle should have opened Lot's eyes that these were not ordinary men and persuaded him to take them seriously.

7. How did the message given to Lot (v.12-13) contrast with the message that had just been given to Abraham up in the hills?

God's message to Abraham was a joyful one. Abraham and Sarah would have son God had promised within a year. Lot received the message that God was going to destroy Sodom and everything in it! God brings joy to His people, but judgment to those who refuse His message and His values.

8. Why was Lot hesitant to leave the city? (v.16)

Sodom was a place that Lot loved seemingly more than his own life. The visitors have to take him by the hand and lead him out of town. Even then, he lingers and begs to be allowed to have salvation in his own way. Instead of taking the warning seriously and being glad that he was alive, he wants more concessions from God so that he can keep as much of the city as possible.

9. Why is it so hard to leave behind things that we know are bad for us?

Answers will vary but may include the fact that we have invested our whole life into them like Lot or that they still have great appeal to us or that we don't take the danger that they present seriously.

10. As you look at the story of Lot in Sodom, what were the consequences of living in Sodom for Lot?

Lot lost everything including his wife, his property and his son in laws. He may have been saved, but his daughters were so filled with Sodom's values that they immorally conceived with their father and gave birth to two sons whose descendants would become enemies of Israel.

20 Even Saints Sin - Gen. 20:1-18

1. Name one mistake that you have done at least twice. How did you handle the consequences of the mistake?

Answers will vary. They might feel embarrassment, guilt or anger at themselves. If no one is willing to share, move on to the story.

2. What did Abraham say about Sarah? Why do you think that he made this mistake a second time? (v.2)

As soon as he went to Gerar, he began to be afraid. He began to walk by his wits and to tell lies. "And there Abraham said of his wife Sarah, she is my sister." (v.2) He was in a foreign land and he forgot the power of his God. He forgot that his God was not limited by area. He even forgot the promise that the Lord had made about Isaac only a few months before (Gen. 18:10). It was as if he moved and left his God behind.

3. What happens because of Abraham's lie? What and whom does Abraham put in jeopardy?

Sarah is 89 and Abimelech wants her for his harem. A simple lie to save Abraham's skin has unanticipated consequences. We can only imagine what would have happened if the king had found her pregnant in his harem or if Isaac would not have been born at all because of this deception. Abraham put all of God's plans in jeopardy with a simple lie. He put his wife and his future in danger because he had not learned from the past.

4. How have you seen lies impact people around you?

Answers will vary but will share the harm that even "white lies" can bring.

5. How does Abimelech's dream show God's concern for all the people involved? (v.3)

God in His mercy intervened to keep His promise regarding Sarah from being destroyed by Abraham's lies. He warns Abimelech that Sarah was married and causes all the other women to become temporarily sterile to make His point. God's warning is a recognition that Abimelech is the victim in this story. God will make the point that Abraham is under His protection but will also restore Abimelech's household to health.

6. Ironically, who is paying the penalty for Abraham's sin? Why did God inflict this penalty?

The Bible doesn't pull any punches. It always tells things just like they are. Our "hero" Abraham looks pretty bad in this text. Isn't it odd that the pagan King Abimelech is the man of integrity in this story? He welcomes Abraham with open arms and is paid for his hospitality with a curse of barrenness. Even God admits "Yes, I know you did this with a clear conscience and so I have kept you from sinning against me." (v.6) Abraham has sinned and the pagan king and his household have paid the price. Ironically, the punishment was given with mercy in mind. God did these things so that the innocent Abimelech would not sin against God's plan without knowing it.

7. In what ways do we often make others suffer to protect ourselves or hide from our sins?

Answers will vary but should include the embarrassment that we cause our family or our friends when we do things that we know are wrong.

8. What is God's command to Abimelech? (v.7) Why do you think that God speaks so clearly to this pagan king?

While God did not defend the sin of his servant, He did bring honor back to Abraham and saves the promise that He made concerning the son that was to be born to Abraham and Sarah. He made Abraham the mediator of restoration and grace so that the king will not punish Abraham for his sin. "Now return the man's wife, for he is a prophet, and he will pray for you and you will live." (v.7) The king will not give Abraham the punishment that he deserves for God has made it clear that Abraham's intercession is the thing that stands between the king and death.

9. How does Abraham try to explain his way out of trouble? (v.11)

Abraham is not even gracious when he is caught in the act of sinning. He blames the very people who have been hurt by his sin. "I said to myself, there is surely no fear of God in this place and they will kill me because of my wife." (v.11) He then excuses his lie because it is half true. God has shown Himself to the king as one who is powerful and merciful. Abraham has shown himself to be a self-centered liar. The good news is that God does not give up on His servant or on the promises that He has made to Abraham.

10. Why do you think that God didn't give up on Abraham at this point? How does that show God can be merciful to His people when they still sin against Him?

Answers will vary but will include the great love that God has for Abraham. Abraham is a child of God and God cares for him just as an earthly father cares for one of his children. God's mercy for Abraham and the lengths that God goes to in order to care for Abraham should show that God will not abandon us.

23 Difficult Choices - Genesis 21: 8-21

1. What motivates you to make the hard decisions like taking a new job or breaking up with a friend?

Answers may vary but will probably include gains that the new direction will take them or a need to get away from something bad in their life. Our natural tendency is to follow the steady course. It usually takes something painful or the offer of a great opportunity for us to want to change.

2. What triggers the problem in the house of Abraham? (v.8) How has a good thing created a big problem?

The problem starts when Isaac is weaned. This was a time of great celebration for it meant that the child was thriving and that the painful time when many infants died was passed. Nowhere do we hear in scripture of a celebration for Ishmael. Isaac has been proclaimed as the child of promise and the heir to everything that Abraham has. Now that claim has become a reality and it doesn't sit well for Ishmael, the older brother.

3. From Sarah's perspective, why must Hagar and Ishmael be sent away? (v10) What do you think that she fears?

Since Jewish children were usually weaned at about age three, Ishmael was probably seventeen at the time of this festival (Gen. 16:16). Ishmael was already mocking his little brother and posed an even greater threat to the safety of Sarah's son as he grew older. Sarah was afraid that this "wild donkey of a man" (Gen. 16:12) who would torment a three-year-old might seriously harm her son as they grew up together. Ishmael seems to be asserting his place because he feels usurped by this younger brother.

4. Who, like Sarah, do you find it hard to get along with? How do you handle it? Is there something you can do

to make things better?

Answers will vary but encourage them to open up to situations even if it is uncomfortable to share names. Let others help them to see Godly ways to deal with the person and to bring healing to the relationship. Help them also be honest about times where, like Sarah, you just have to say goodbye to someone who poses a danger to your life or future.

5. What is at the heart of Abraham's distress? (v.11)

The text tells us that Abraham is distressed because "it concerned with his son". Ishmael was Abraham's son as much as Isaac was. Little Isaac was only a few years old while Abraham had watched Ishmael grow up for seventeen years and had grown attached to his son. Sending him away would be hard. One wonders if part of the grief was due, in part, to the fact that Ishmael came about only because Abraham had not trusted God. God had never accepted Ishmael as the heir and Abraham now saw the trouble that his first son was causing and the threat that Ishmael could be to God's promises.

6. How would you feel if you had to send your son away?

Answers will vary but explore how members of the group would feel if they got married a second time and an older child was a threat to a younger child from the second marriage. How would they feel if they had to send the first child off to live with the first wife or another relative? What behaviors would make it prudent to send the older child away?

7. What wisdom does God share with Abraham? (v.12) What reason does God give for making this hard choice?

God tells Abraham to listen to his wife. The character of Ishmael has begun to be revealed. Sarah sees what God described concerning Ishmael before he was born. This would be a man whose "hand will be against everyone" and who "live in hostility toward all his brothers." (Gen 16:12). Sarah has a right to be afraid of Ishmael. God also puts some perspective on the problem. He stresses to Abraham that He never approved of the plan that Abram and Sarai had for providing their own heir. Isaac alone will receive the blessings of the promises. It may be a heartbreak to Abraham, but Ishmael cannot share in the promise that God had given to him.

8. While Ishmael was outside of God's covenant and promise, what assurances does God give to Hagar about her son? (v.18) Why would God bless this troublesome teen?

God tells Hagar that He will make the boy into a great nation. It is a repetition of the promise that God made to Abraham before Isaac was born. (Gen. 17:20-22) At that time, God promised Abraham that He would bless Ishmael and make him the father of a great nation including 12 rulers. All of these promises were for Abraham's benefit. This was his son and it was a comfort to know that God would watch over and bless Ishmael as well as Isaac.

9. In choosing Isaac over Ishmael, was God being fair?

Answers will vary, but it is important for the group to remember that Ishmael was conceived when Abram and Sarai took matters into their own hands because they doubted God's promise. God had promised that Isaac would be born at the right time. God's choice had always been Isaac for he was the son of promise. God's mercy is shown in His gracious promises to Ishmael. God did not discard him but gave Ishmael great promises for his future.

10. What difficult choices have you faced or are you facing right now? What does the example of Abraham show you about trusting the Lord's direction in those decisions?

Answers will vary, but the wisdom of God's advice is seen in considering the other options. Isaac and Ishmael could have been forced to live together which would have meant constant conflict or Isaac could have been driven away by Ishmael which would have destroyed God's promises. God knew that the only solution was for Ishmael to leave. We can trust his direction because He sees clearly the best option for all those involved.

26 Entrusting Your Children to God - Gen. 22:1-19

1. What possession or person would be hardest for you to give up?

Answers will vary but let them relate their situation to Abraham's decision to give up the most important person in his life.

2. What command does God give to Abraham in verse 2? What is at stake for Abraham if Isaac dies?

God came to him with a command that no one wants to hear. "Take your son, your only son, Isaac. . . sacrifice him there as a burnt offering" (v.2) It was a test to see how much Abraham loved his God. Abraham was being asked to sacrifice the greatest thing that God had given him because he trusted the Lord. Abraham had waited for 25 years for this son. He knew that all the promises of God depended on Isaac. If Isaac was gone, there would be no descendants as numerous as the stars and no one to inherit the land. Surely, Isaac's life was more precious to Abraham than his own life.

3. How does Abraham respond to this command? (v.3)

Trials can be used to teach us to obey and follow God's commands. "Early the next morning Abraham got up and saddled his donkey" (v.3) If God is to teach us, we must be in the right place. Abraham could have refused to take the journey and the lesson would never have happened. Instead, he makes a painful journey to Moriah as the Lord commands. It was at Moriah where the lesson was to take place. We often think that we have a right to demand that God should solve our problems and help us with our needs on our schedule. Yet only when we have obeyed the Lord and are at His place and time will we find the real solutions.

4. What do you picture Abraham thinking as he hears and responds to this command? How would you feel if you were asked you to give up something precious to you?

Answers will vary, but might include fear, doubts about God's love, and anger. Give them a chance to express how hard this would be and why it would be so difficult.

5. How far away is Moriah (v.4)? How would this make the test more difficult?

God didn't ask Abraham to take his son and sacrifice him immediately. It would have been easier to strike Isaac down quickly while you had your nerve. Abraham was called to make a long journey to the sacred mountain. It was "on the third day Abraham looked up and saw the place in the distance." (v.4) The three-day journey gave Abraham plenty of time to turn back and refuse what seemed to be a cruel request. Here, there would be no wife or servants to stop him from completing the task. Here he would have to fight only his own desires as he sacrificed his precious son.

6. Many think that Isaac is a teenager at the time of the test. What question does he ask (v.7) and how does Abraham answer (v.8)?

Isaac asks where the lamb is for the burnt offering. Abraham replies that God will provide the burnt offering. Remember that Abraham could not have offered Isaac without Isaac's consent and cooperation. Isaac, as the bearer of the wood, is the stronger of the two. As a young man, he is also faster than his father. Clearly, Isaac is strong enough and big enough to resist or subdue his father. In a way, this is a question of his obedience, too.

7. On the mountain, how does Abraham show the depth of his faith? (v.10) Do you think that Abraham would have really killed his son?

In the end, he was willing to give back to the Lord the greatest gift that he had received. "Then he reached out his hand and took the knife to slay his son." (v.10) He believed in the promises of God so much that he trusted that God would give his son back to him somehow. What God would do with the sacrifice, Abraham did not know. He could only trust God and know that his God had always loved him and would keep the promises He had made about this son. There may be people in the group who do not believe that Abraham would have killed his son. Don't argue with them, just ask them why they feel the way that they do. Such a strong faith is often hard to understand.

8. When does God stop the sacrifice (v.11) and what can we learn from God's timing?

God chooses the time. Only at the last minute does the Lord provide for His servant. The lesson has had its full effect. God could have stopped Abraham after one day of the journey or even at the foot of the mountain. Yet, it was only when the lesson was complete that the Lord provided an answer. He wanted Abraham to know and act as if he believed that the Lord would provide the lamb for the burnt offering. God will not allow us to quit in the middle of His trials but wants us to grow fully from the experience.

9. How does God provide the sacrifice as Abraham said he would (v.13)?

When the time and place are right, God often provides an ordinary answer. God could have sent an angel down from heaven with a lamb or miraculously made one appear before Abraham. Yet, God often does things in a way that seem ordinary. In this case, He simply allowed a ram to get caught in a bush by its horns. Some would call it coincidence, it was so unobtrusive. Yet we know that it was God's way of providing. Abraham needed an animal for the altar that he had built, and God arranged for him to have one at the very moment that he needed it. God often uses the ordinary things of life to provide help at just the right moment.

10 What does Abraham's example teach us about trusting the Lord enough to obey Him in every situation?

Answers may vary but include the power of faith and the love and mercy of God. Life can be tough, but God can handle anything that the world throws at us. We just have to wait for His time and His solutions. If we stop trusting because God takes too long, we can keep the blessing and answer of God from coming.

30 Knowing When to Say Yes - Gen. 24:15-67

1. How do you know when to say yes to a decision?

Answers may vary, but often involve weighing the pros and cons and a lot of prayers. We may also ask the opinion of people that we respect who can give unbiased views. Finally, we consider how it will impact our family and extended family. If there is time, let someone in the group share how they made such a decision.

2. What problems would have been created if Isaac had married a Canaanite? How does marrying a relative negate those problems?

To marry a Canaanite would have caused a division in the family. The children of Isaac were to conquer the people around them at some point and take the land. A Canaanite mother would have complicated that and could have even introduced a pagan God into the family.

3. What sign does the servant ask from the Lord? (v.14) How does this show the servant's trust in the Lord and his willingness to allow the Lord to make the choice?

He prayed to the Lord, suggesting a test of hospitality and service. "May it be that when I say to a girl, please let down your jar that I may have a drink. . . let her be the one you have chosen for your servant Isaac." This is a test of humility asking the Lord to choose the right woman. The bride of Isaac is to be the Lord's choice. He believes so strongly in the promise that the Lord has made that he expects the Lord will direct him to the right woman. He will not act rashly or try to find her. He will wait patiently for the Lord to reveal His choice.

4. Others ask for signs in scripture like Gideon in the book of Judges. What sign might you ask for if you were ill or if you were asked to take over a ministry at church?

Answers will vary but might include an opportunity opening up or the council of a friend.

5. How did Rebekah react when she saw the need of the stranger? (v.19) How do the qualities that she exhibits show that she is an exceptional young woman?
God more than answered the servant's prayer with the arrival of Rebekah. "After she had given him a drink, she said, I'll draw water for your camels too." (v.19) As he watched the young woman water the camels, he may have wondered if his mission was already successful. He had asked for a sign from the Lord and the woman showed kindness and compassion in exactly the way that the servant had asked for in his request. Not only was she the granddaughter of Abraham's brother Nahor and a virgin, but she was also very beautiful.

6. If you ask for a sign, how might you know that it is a sign from God and not from another source?

Answers will vary, but the answer will be in line with the Bible and with the skills that the Lord has given you. It should also be something that will not expect you to sin (tell a white lie, dishonor God, or react in anger, etc.) or expect you to do something that is impossible for you.

7. How does the family react to this proposal from Abraham through his servant? (v.55)

Rebekah's brother and mother were willing for her to become Isaac's wife, but they had a condition. "Let the girl remain with us ten days or so, then you may go."(v.55). This was a natural request since the parents would want to spend as much time as possible with her and perhaps even invite the neighbors to celebrate with them. Of course, they were delighted with the wealth the servant gave them, which was probably the marriage dowry. They may have also still had questions about the marriage and concerns about Rebekah moving so far away.

8. What is Rebekah's answer when the servant is in a hurry to have an answer and return to Palestine? (v.58) What do you think led her to this answer?

He asked that they let Rebekah make the choice. What did she think? "So, they called Rebekah and asked her, will you go with this man? I will go, she said." (v.58) What motivated Rebekah to make the right decision? It seems that she heard the word about Isaac and believed it. She also saw the proof of his greatness, generosity, and wealth. She knew that she could weigh the pros and cons for several days, but ultimately her answer was just to trust God.

9. What was at stake in her answer? What would the rest of the Bible look like if she had said no?

The events showed that God had chosen Rebekah to be the wife of Isaac. Yet, God did not force her to answer. It was up to Rebekah to make this choice for herself. She had to trust the Lord and be willing to put her life and her future in God's hands. It was all about saying yes to God's opportunity. The minute she said yes, she became part of God's plan of salvation for the whole world. If she had said no, she would have been forgotten and God would have had to choose another so that He could honor His promise to Abraham. The opportunity was great, and we remember her today because of her choice.

10. What have you learned about difficult decisions?

Answers will vary. God does allow us to make the wrong decision, but He will give us all the encouragement that we should need to trust Him and follow Him. God had obviously prepared Rebekah for this answer and gave her all the signs that showed that she had the opportunity for something great. God also allows us to ask for signs or seek the advice of other

Christians so that we follow His will and not our own.

31 Full of Years - Gen. 25:1-19

1. What is your dream for your retirement years?

Answers vary, but Old age doesn't have to mean empty years. The Lord continues to walk beside us and to bless us even as we age. He has tasks for us to do and a life for us to live. Many people retire at age 65 with no plan for the future other than a desire not to work. A better plan might be to slow down but use retirement to take on a new career or to do something you never had the time to do before.

2. Abraham was 137 years old when Sarah died. How did Abraham live his life after the death of Sarah? (v.1)

Sarah's death (Gen. 23:1) didn't seem to slow this patriarch down. He remarried and had six more children including Midian, the father of the Midianites of Moses' time. God continued to bless Abraham all his life. Just because Sarah had died, or Isaac was now on his own did not mean that life was over. He defines for us what it means to have a full and productive life.

3. With the six other children, Abraham had eight children with three women. How is his estate divided (v.5) Why is this division?

When life was ending, Abraham made sure that the torch did pass to Isaac. "Abraham left everything he owned to Isaac. But while he was still living, he gave gifts to the sons of his concubines." (v.5-6) Perhaps the Lord had given Abraham a clue that the end was near. Maybe it just seemed time as he came close to being 175 years old. He had followed the Lord for the last 100 years. He wanted to make sure that the legacy the Lord had given him would not be in danger. He gave everything to Isaac for God had named Isaac the son of the promise.

308   32 Days with Abraham

4. What happened to Keturah's children? What might Abraham be afraid of?

The six sons of Keturah were given gifts and ultimately sent away to the east. No one was to challenge Isaac. Nothing was to get in the way of God's covenant line. The descendants of Midian would fight the Jews in Moses' day (Numbers 22) and in Gideon's day (Judges 6-7). Many of the relatives of the Jews like the Edomites, the Moabites, and the Midianites became enemies of the Jews. Sending these children away gave the nation of Israel time to grow before they were challenged.

5. How is the life of Abraham described in verse 8? How is that a great compliment to this patriarch?

The blessing of the Lord brought both quantity and quality to his life. "Then Abraham breathed his last and died at a good old age, an old man and full of years and he was gathered to his people." (v.8) He is described as dying "full of years". There was quality to his life. This was not a wilted man living on the charity of others. This was a man who could proudly look back on what the Lord had done. He could remember his walk with the Lord and the joys that the Lord had brought. He was a man who could look around and see the wealth that the Lord had given him with large herds and a large family. He was also a man who could look ahead confident that all of God's promises were going to be fulfilled.

6. How would you like your life to be described at your death? What characteristics do you think are most important?

Answers will vary but may include a family that loves and respects them or a life that made a difference to others. A good exercise here (if it seems appropriate for your group) would be to ask what each person wants their close friends to say about them at their death or what they want on their tombstone.

7. What do you think made Abraham's life a success? How will that influence how you live?

Abraham gives us the real measure of success. Abraham could joyfully look back at his walk with the Lord and feel blessed at all that God has done for him. He then could look forward and build on that foundation by serving the Lord and others until the end of life. The full life of Abraham came because God was there every day. Abraham had learned to walk and talk with God. Abraham had learned to depend on God and to live in faith. Answers will vary as the group talks about one thing that they have learned from Abraham that will influence their lives.

8. Where is Abraham buried? (v.9)

The cave was to the east of Mamre, or Hebron and was purchased by Abraham as a burial place for his wife Sarah. (Gen. 23:19). Today the modern city of el-Khalil (Hebron) is built up around the site of Machpelah. The site of the cave can still be visited today. It was once protected by a Christian church but is now marked by a Moslem mosque.

9. What do you admire most about the life of Abraham? What would you like to emulate in your life?

Answers will vary but should focus on the relationship that Abraham had with the Lord and the blessings that the Lord brought to Abraham because of his faith. To be like Abraham means to be one who is growing in their relationship with the Lord and living a life of obedience to God and service to others.

About the author

Rev. Mark Etter has been a pastor for over thirty years and is currently the pastor of a Lutheran Church in Northern Kentucky. He graduated from Concordia Seminary in St. Louis, Missouri with a Master of Divinity degree and from Illinois State University with a Bachelor of Music Education degree. Mark has published several books of Adult Bible studies and numerous devotions and youth studies with Concordia Publishing House in St. Louis. He has served the greater church as a pastoral coach, evangelism chairman, and circuit counselor. He is married to Joan and they have three grown children who live in Kentucky and Indiana.

In His spare time, he loves to go camping across the United States so that he can enjoy the national and state parks and learn from the many historic sites of our nation. He still uses his musical training as he leads the praise team at his church and sings in the choir. His life goal is to create a series of 32-day devotions that will open sections of the scripture to others so people can be closer to Christ by the power of the stories and teachings of the Bible. He enjoys seeing people discover how great our God really is so that they can love God and live in God's blessings. He would love to hear how this devotion helped you or hear any suggestions for future books. Feel free to contact Mark by email at 32daysdevotions@gmail.com.

Chronology of Abraham

Biblical Event	Bible Ref.	Abraham Age	Isaac Age
Entrance into Canaan	12:4	75	
Ishmael born to Abram	16:16	86	
Isaac born	21:5	100	0
Abraham offers his son on Mt. Moriah	22	115?	15?
Sarah dies	23:1	137	37
Isaac marries Rebekah	25:20	140	40
Jacob and Esau are born	25:26	160	60
Abraham dies	25:7	175	75

Please visit www.32daysdevotions.com for more information and study resources.

Other titles from Higher Ground Books & Media:

Wise Up to Rise Up by Rebecca Benston

A Path to Shalom by Steen Burke

Overcomer by Forrest Henslee

Miracles: I Love Them by Forest Godin

32 Days with Christ's Passion by Mark Etter

Knowing Affliction and Doing Recovery by John

Baldasare

Out of Darkness by Stephen Bowman

The Magic Egg by Linda Phillipson

The Tin Can Gang by Chuck David

Whobert the Owl by Mya C. Benston

Add these titles to your collection today!

http://highergroundbooksandmedia.com

www.ingramcontent.com/pod-product-compliance
Lightning Source LLC
LaVergne TN
LVHW011344080426
835511LV00005B/121